The #1 Sales Team

Superior Techniques for
Maximum Performance

Stephan Schiffman

BUSINESS

Adams Media
Avon, Massachusetts

Dedication

To Martha F. Schiffman
In loving memory

Copyright © 2006, Stephan Schiffman
All rights reserved. This book, or parts thereof, may not be reproduced in any form
without permission from the publisher; exceptions are made for brief excerpts used
in published reviews.

Published by
Adams Media, an F+W Publications Company
57 Littlefield Street
Avon, MA 02322
www.adamsmedia.com

ISBN: 1-59337-494-1

Printed in the United States of America.

J I H G F E D C B A

Library of Congress Cataloging-in-Publication Data
available from publisher.

This publication is designed to provide accurate and authoritative information with
regard to the subject matter covered. It is sold with the understanding that the publisher
is not engaged in rendering legal, accounting, or other professional advice. If legal advice
or other expert assistance is required, the services of a competent professional person
should be sought.

—From a *Declaration of Principles* jointly adopted by a Committee of the American Bar
Association and a Committee of Publishers and Associations

Many of the designations used by manufacturers and sellers to distinguish their product
are claimed as trademarks. Where those designations appear in this book and Adams
Media was aware of a trademark claim, the designations have been printed with initial
capital letters.

Interior design and composition by
Electronic Publishing Services, Inc. Tennessee

This book is available at quantity discounts for bulk purchases.
For information, please call 1-800-872-5627.

Contents

Part IV
Are They Implementing the Skills? / 119

Part V
Hiring—and Keeping Together—the #1 Sales Team / 193

— Appendix —
Resources for Sales Managers / 231

Acknowledgments

———————

The first and most important acknowledgment I can make is to the many sales managers I have worked with over the last three decades.

If you are a sales manager, then you already know what I'm talking about when I say that you have what has to be one of the most difficult jobs in the professional world. Sales representatives go out and sell each and every day, and before too long, they see the results, whether those results are good or bad. Some days are good, and some days are bad, but at least salespeople know what they've done, and they know the reasoning behind the decisions they've made.

It's different for sales managers. You as the manager must do your job with the team . . . and then sit back and wait to see whether anything you've done has actually worked. How long you have to wait usually depends on the industry you're working in, but regardless of the length of time, it's usually a frustrating and difficult period. The truth is that there really isn't that much you can do when the reps are actually out in the field. You may wish you could always be "where the action is," and you may actually go out on sales calls as time permits, but for the most part, you *aren't* by the side of your salespeople when the actual purchase decisions are made. You can only gauge what's going on based on the reports, formal or otherwise, that you may (or may not) receive along the way.

Often, sales are flat or down even after you have worked with someone very closely; this may be because the salesperson is unresponsive, because the value of each unit has dropped, or for any of a dozen other reasons. Ultimately, all you can do is learn to coach salespeople effectively—that is, learn to affect the factors that *are* under your control, as opposed to fretting about the factors that aren't. And that's what this book is all about.

My gratitude and respect goes out to the sales managers; this book is written for *you*, and not for the representative. There are many books that cover the art of selling, but very few books on sales coaching. In this book, I have tried to cover it all, from the most basic ideas to the most advanced techniques you can use to monitor and improve your team. What I have learned about this subject, I have learned from working with able professionals, and so I acknowledge, with deep gratitude, the insights and strategies I have developed over the years with the help of the thousands of sales managers I've worked with. The chapters that follow are designed to give you some important insights into your staff and yourself . . . and to guide you quickly into the world of effective sales management, so that you can pick up in a matter of weeks or months (or however long it takes you to finish this book) what I had to learn over decades of working with seasoned sales management professionals. In addition, I want to acknowledge *you*, for investing your time and energy in the strategies you will find here, and I wish you all the best.

I must note, too, that this book could not have been written without the help of many people at D.E.I. Management Group. First, as always, I thank Brandon Toropov, who helped me throughout the project with the transcription and editing. I am also grateful to Michele Reisner, who gave generously of her time, combed through our training materials archive, and reviewed the final text patiently. Many thanks go to Steve Bookbinder, a star trainer, and always a friend. Thanks go out to Martha Rios and David Rivera, who somehow manage to solve the vast majority of problems in our business before they happen, and to Ben Alpert, Alan Koval and Surendra Sewsankar.

At Adams Media, I am indebted to Gary Krebs, Danielle Chiotti, and Shoshanna Grossman. I also want to thank my agent Stephanie Kip Rostan at Levine Greenberg Communications. Without the support and assistance of these good people, this book would never have seen the light of day.

I also have a whole new group of people to thank, namely those who own and operate our franchise organizations, which as of this writing stretch from California to Massachusetts, and from Dublin to Saudi Arabia. Our franchisees have inspired me as a person, and they have given me new perspective on the many issues that I write about.

Finally, my unending gratitude, and my love, go out to Anne, Jennifer, and Daniele.

Introduction

If you're like most of the sales managers with whom I've worked over the years, you're eager to find strategies that will help you to deliver results sooner, rather than later. So, I'll get right to the point.

This book is about a single problem—with many possible causes.

The problem is easy to describe, but it takes a great deal of practice and dedication to solve.

The problem is this: If time is represented as a horizontal line . . . and income is represented as a vertical line . . . then the ideal performance pattern for the salespeople that we hire *should*, in a perfect world, look just like this:

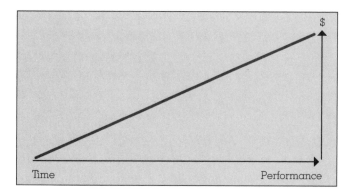

That's the ideal. In the real world, though, you and I know that doesn't happen.

That's our problem as sales managers. Why doesn't that happen? And what can we do about it?

Read on.

PART

I

The Basics for Managers

If they know what the job is (and God knows they should) . . .

*. . . if they know how to do the job (and God knows they're
supposed to) . . .*

*. . . and if they are implementing what they know (and God
knows they ought to be) . . .*

. . . how come they aren't hitting quota?

What Really Works?

Good sales managers have to focus continuously on a pragmatic question: "What's really going to work?"

Over the past quarter-century or so, I've worked with more than half a million salespeople, professionals who have sold in just about every industry you can imagine. And during that quarter-century, what started out as a one-man business has turned into an international sales training and consulting operation with offices all over the United States, in Canada, Europe, the Middle East, and South Africa. So apparently something we're doing really works.

Specifically, the ideas on coaching and managing salespeople that appear in this book do work. We know they work because we've trained managers in all kinds of companies to implement what you're about to read—managers whose job it is to get people to sell software, managers whose job it is to get people to refinance homes, managers whose job it is to get people to switch their garbage pickup service, managers whose job it is to get people to sell lubricants, managers whose job it is to get people to sell cellular phones. Just about every kind of sales manager you can think of has used what's between these covers to increase sales.

To understand how I coach salespeople, it helps to understand how I *interview* people who apply to my own company for a job in our sales department.

So, let me walk you through what happens in a typical sales interview at my company.

"Tell Me about Your Numbers"

When I interview someone who wants to sell for my organization, I will look the person straight in the eye, and after establishing a little rapport with some basic pleasantries, I will ask, "Tell me about your numbers."

Nothing more. Nothing less. That's my first important question. It usually produces a blank stare and a long pause.

What happens next is the point at which I find out whether this person is interested in thinking about selling the way that I do.

> By the way, if you're familiar with my training material and my books, some of the following material may sound familiar to you, but please keep reading anyway. I always add some twists to these books for people who've read my stuff or heard me speak before—and I guarantee there are more twists in this book than in any other of my books. Don't skip these opening chapters!

If the person says, "Well, last year I earned so-many dollars," and then insists on discussing salary—no matter how tactfully I try to steer the subject to other numbers—I know there is a potential problem.

If, on the other hand, the person *asks what I mean* by "numbers" . . . or talks meaningfully about his or her daily activity benchmarks, then I know there is a pretty good chance I am talking to somebody who represents a good fit with what we do at D.E.I.

To explain what I meant by "tell me about your numbers," I will usually say something like the following.

> "Let me tell you what I do each and every day that I am not training. Every day that I am not actually in front of a group, I will pick up the phone fifteen times and dial it—that is, I will try to reach out to fifteen new people I have not talked to before.
>
> "Of those fifteen dials, I will end up having seven conversations with people who could conceivably give me an appointment.
>
> "And of those seven discussions, I will set one new first appointment with a decision-maker. By decision-maker, I mean someone who can move me forward in the sales cycle. I do not set appointments with receptionists, and I also do not abandon the company if I cannot immediately reach the president.
>
> "So those are the daily numbers: fifteen, seven, one.
>
> "Those are my numbers. And that is what I meant when I asked *you* what *your* numbers were. Each day, you do something that produces sales somewhere down the line. You have some kind of numbers to monitor. And the salespeople we like to work with make a habit of measuring their daily numbers in the same way, day after day."

If you think I stop talking to the applicant at that stage, and let the other person do some talking, you're mistaken. When I talk to prospects, I am always looking for ways to get them to open up and talk to me during the first few minutes of the conversation. When I talk to *job applicants*, however, I'm looking for opportunities to share my own philosophy of selling.

So, I don't stop there. I keep talking.

> "Let's examine the process a little further. If I manage to do that every day—fifteen, seven, and one—that means I will set five new appointments each week. However, since my sale typically requires more than one visit, the total number of *visits* that I go on each week is *larger* than five.
>
> "In fact, that number is eight. Typically, I will go on five first-time visits during an average week, and follow through with three follow-through visits during that same week. So that's a total of eight meetings.
>
> "As it happens, my closing ratio is eight to one. In other words, for every eight visits that I go on, I will produce one new sale. I do that fifty weeks a year, which means I produce fifty new sales a year. That's my lifestyle number—that adds up to the dollar figure I want to hit. That dollar figure is *why* I make the fifteen dials every day. So let's take a look at the numbers and see how they stack up."

It is at this point that I pull out a legal pad and set up the following diagram:

15:7:1

8:1

50 ($)

Notice that what we're talking about here are *ratios*. How many dials does it take me to create a first appointment? How many visits do I have to go on in order to create a sale? And so on.

The #1 Sales Team

Here's the Twist

As I say, if you've ever heard me speak in front of a group, or read one of my books, that explanation of fifteen, seven, and one that you just heard probably sounds familiar. (I don't apologize for that, by the way. Important points are worth repeating, especially when it comes to salespeople making money for their families.)

Nevertheless, here's the part that's probably not familiar to you, the twist, the part that will make you glad you decided to keep reading a couple of minutes ago. Here's where the new stuff for managers comes in.

What I want you to notice is that there are three *levels* to my activity . . .

15:7:1

8:1

50 ($)

. . . and that those three levels require three very different skill sets.

On the first level, the appointment-setting level, what is required is *energy*. Once you get the technique down, you really can set a significant number of first appointments on enthusiasm alone. You won't necessarily get many *second* appointments, but that's a different story. Since first appointments drive the sales process, the energy part of the equation is extremely important.

On the second level, the level where I move the appointments forward to and get closer to closure, I take advantage of my own *selling skills*. That means I do a good enough job of gathering information and presenting to actually close some deals. That's an important skill, too.

And in the third level, my goal is to hit that lifestyle number I've established for myself. The best (though not the only) way to do that is to retain as much as possible of the value I ask for in my proposal to the prospect. In other words, I have a clear duty to try to **defend my company's value**, to close deals that are close to the price that I set out in the proposal that I built for a prospective customer. Now, it is a fact of sales life that over time, that number is not going to equal exactly 100 percent of my request in the proposals that I develop, but it is also a fact of sales life that I will always want to make that number as high a percentage as humanly possible. Another way of saying this is that my proposals are "good" to the degree that they (1) offer packages, pricing, and timing that prospects can agree with, and (2) deliver a margin for my organization and commission dollars to me. This final level requires not the pure energy necessary to deliver appointments, as in the first level, nor even the information-gathering and presenting ability necessary to move the sale forward in the second level. This third level requires a different set of skills that we can call *value retention skills.*

When you put it all together it looks like this:

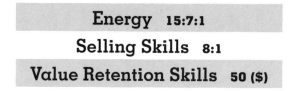

Energy 15:7:1

Selling Skills 8:1

Value Retention Skills 50 ($)

These, then, are the three skill levels—energy, selling skills, and value retention skills—that I make a habit of monitoring in myself . . . and in the salespeople who work with me. They're what make commission checks happen, and they determine the size of those checks. The actual size of the checks isn't as interesting to me as a familiarity with the process that delivers the checks.

When I ask someone who wants to work for our organization, "Can you tell me about your numbers?" I'm not really asking about money. I'm not that interested in how much he or she earned last year, although that is good supplementary information.

What I am truly interested in is his or her ability to **notice and measure daily activity benchmarks in each of these three areas.**

The Turning Point

I've been talking up until now about *daily* activity. But sales careers don't play out over a few days or weeks. (Or at least, managers don't think they should.) Sales careers play out over months and years.

Let me tell you what's probably playing out right on your sales staff.

A manager is always looking at two things in sales. The first, as you've gathered, is time. And the second thing is results. That's the dollar line, which is vertical.

So, a sales representative starts out and is expected to generate a certain amount of money in a certain period.

And, as I mentioned in the introduction, this is the ideal kind of configuration:

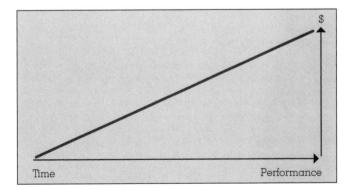

There's a saying I use when discussing the progress a person can make in his or her sales career: "Expectation drives achievement and rewards!" That is true. What the person expects has a great deal to do with his or her performance.

What actually happens in the beginning is that the people we hire start out very excited. Salespeople expect that they are going to keep moving straight up to the top of that "$" line.

They think they're going to own the Learjet and be president of the company. Whatever their goal is, at the beginning they believe that they're going to achieve it, and that's only natural.

So, you start out, and you're at a certain point when you're going to say, "Look at me! I'm gung-ho; I'm doing it; I'm doing it. Watch out, world!"

But what eventually happens is there comes a point in your career when the excitement that you had, in terms of doing the work, isn't quite at that level anymore. This is what we call the **corporate career turning point.**

And, in this period, a decision point happens.

It's the point when people suddenly realize that the initial achievement, the fun, and the expectation that they had just isn't the same anymore, and they're probably not going to have that Learjet. And (speaking frankly), some salespeople decide that their lawn is a lot more interesting than their job is.

This is the point when the largest percentage of salespeople "checks out." They level off and stop investing quite so much excitement and enthusiasm in their career.

Now look what happens. It's at this point that people start to level off. Their achievements start to resemble the gray line in the following diagram, the one that quickly changes from going up to going nowhere in particular. And they never reach the goal they associated with that third vertical line, which is where we would like them to be by that point.

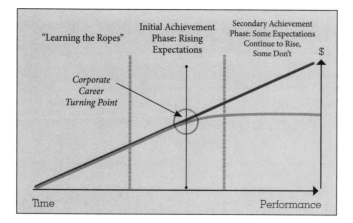

Believe me, this is happening to somebody on your team. It isn't that there is no more prospecting to be done; it's that people aren't motivated in the sixth month of their career in the same way they were in the first month, or that they aren't motivated in the third year of their career as they were in the first year. (It all depends on the cycle for the individual company.)

It isn't that there aren't more people to see. It's just that the representative has made that long climb and hasn't been able to keep the enthusiasm level at the point it needs to be to sustain the momentum toward the initial goal. Now it's gotten to a critical point in his life when he's saying he would rather be a mentor than be mentored. He would rather counsel people than be counseled. Whether they want to emerge as mentors, some salespeople start to lose focus. They start to focus on everything else *but* improving their own level of sales performance.

5 What Can You Do?

It's difficult to get the person back to that initial phase of excitement. What you can do, however, is to get the person to be more productive for a longer period.

And that's what this book is all about—giving salespeople and managers benchmarks, so they can extend the line. You can make the plateau happen *after* it otherwise would. You can make the career turning point happen noticeably later in the career cycle.

> If you use the ideas in this book to train, reinforce, and coach your team, you can extend the average productive lifespan of your salespeople.

If you follow the advice in this book, you'll find that, rather than fighting or quitting, your salespeople are going to be productive for *x* number of months or years longer than they would otherwise be. That should be one of your most important objectives: to work with this person to extend his or her productive life within the organization.

If you can extend the period of rising expectations, you can get somebody to be productive longer. How much longer? That is going to depend on the selling environment, on the product or service, and, to a very large degree, on you.

Here's another way to look at it. If you're a salesperson, there is a possibility that you are, at some point, going to get frustrated, and you are going to give up—either quit mentally (and just show up out of force of habit and stop trying), or quit outright.

When will that take place? For some salespeople, it takes place after a number of years, which is a career crisis related to selling. For other salespeople, however—namely, the new hires who go bad—this process plays out after just a few weeks or months. That's typically a job crisis. The person quits right before he or she is about to start making the real money.

> Many sales managers lose salespeople they shouldn't, because the person leaves before she really gets the hang of the job.

Have you ever had that happen on your team? Have you ever, for instance, had somebody quit who complained that the "territory stinks"? The brand-new person you gave the responsibility of developing that territory swears that it is flat, unproductive, played out, or whatever. This new salesperson has been complaining about the territory for months and has bailed out: "I'm not making money here." That person is gone.

You put somebody new in the territory, and the most amazing thing happens. All of a sudden, the first two months of this new person working that territory, there's explosive growth! Everybody goes nuts over the territory. Suddenly, that territory is a superb place to make a living. And why is that? Because all the stuff that was on the edge was about to break for the salesperson who left. All that work ends up being translated into somebody else's commission check. Many of the new salespeople we hire quit at *exactly* the point their work is about to pay off!

So, we have two problems. Number one, the *manager* does not make it clear to the salesperson exactly how much work is required to succeed. And number two, the *salesperson* doesn't make enough of an effort to find out when the payoff is going to start to happen.

In a perfect world, both would do that job, but in the world we live in, neither person does anything. The rep gets disgusted and that affects her daily activity. Of course, that process of getting disgusted affects the performance and makes it even easier to get *more* disgusted with the job and eventually be discouraged enough to leave.

If the salesperson knew exactly what the timing usually looked like, what the cause-and-effect relationship in this job typically was between activity and results, would she quit at this stage? I don't think so.

Peer Pressure and Family Pressure

There is yet another factor that inhibits people from succeeding during the early going, and that is the **peer pressure** that they experience during the all-important "ramp-up period."

The new representative comes into the company and says, "This is my shot. I'm going to make the most of it. And it's going to work. I'm going to do great." The salesperson (let's say we're talking about a man) is optimistic about his prospects.

But if the company is not well known, something strange happens to undercut that optimism.

He goes home and talks about the new job at the next family cookout or barbecue. If the person is young, he probably says to his mom and dad, "Hey, I got a job with the WeirdTec Company."

Now, the WeirdTec Company may be a good company to work for, but Mom and Dad do not know that company. They have never heard of it. So, Mom and Dad say, "What the heck is the WeirdTec Company? Never heard of it."

At that point, the new salesperson says, "Well, the WeirdTec Company is a great company, here is what you should know about it . . . *Yada yada yada . . .* This is my shot, I'm going to make the most of it. And Mom, Dad, it's all going to work out. I'm going to do great there. In fact, I'm going to make a million dollars." But, of course, Mom and Dad have their doubts.

At the same time, the person's peers may be making more money, even though they are doing less work. They may have a better job or simply be selling a more popular product. But the bottom line is they are outearning our salesperson, maybe because they're working in jobs that don't have a ramp-up period, as most sales jobs do.

So, people have this peer-pressure issue, not only from close friends who may be doing "better" than they are initially, but also from family members who need to be convinced that the person made the right choice in the first place.

And, by the way, even experienced reps have peer pressure, perhaps along the following lines: "When are you going to become president?" Or the peer pressure could be: "Did you close a sale today? Did you make the President's Club today?" There are all kinds of peer pressure.

7 Product Identification

Another factor that affects the salesperson's performance is what I call **product identification**. This happens if you are selling a product that does not excite you. My firm works with a company that is one of the biggest companies in the United States, and its mission is hauling trash. You can make a lot of money at that company, but it is not necessarily something you want to share at your parents' fiftieth wedding anniversary, that you just got a new job at a company that hauls garbage.

Eventually the sales representative may get that kind of pressure, too, and he starts thinking, "Gee, what am I doing this for?"

We worked with a person not too long ago who sold ball bearings. He made a lot of money, but he simply did not like telling people that he sold ball bearings for a living! He did not want to admit it. I do not know why he had a problem with it, but he did. But he would tell people he was a lawyer instead of a salesperson for a ball bearing company. Go figure.

For whatever reason, the point is that it happens. So, when there is this peer pressure, often the rep simply says, "You know what? I am done here." He moves on to someplace else. He is on his way to find someplace new, someplace he will make money, someplace he will not have to deal with peer pressure, someplace he will be proud to talk about. The irony is he probably will face some variation of the same problems all over again.

Your problem as a manager is finding a way to get your people to *stay long enough to make a meaningful contribution to your company* and to *extend the long-term productive life of those team members who do stay with you.*

Okay. How are you going to do that?

Passion Without Discipline Equals Chaos

8

When I ask managers how they plan to get their employees to stay until they are productive, and how they can extend their period of high productivity, many say, "Well, I just have to keep them pumped up." I have a problem with that.

Some people believe one thing alone makes success in sales possible: Passion!

When I conduct a sales coaching program in front of an audience of managers, I ask them to name someone who exemplifies their idea of passion and who puts that passion to work in a positive way. Most of the time, the same person shows up at the top of the list. Can you guess who it is?

If you're like most of the people I train, you thought of Michael Jordan when the word *passion* was used as a characteristic of a famous person. Why is that? I think it is because Jordan's level of success, which propelled the National Basketball Association to heights of popularity it had never reached, really was something extraordinary—not unlike, say, the early years of Beatlemania in the 1960s. Jordan did not just exhibit passion; he lived it. But what people sometimes overlook is that he combined that passion with a discipline so steely and so powerful that it made him an icon in American sports *and* popular culture.

Before we go any farther, I want to take a moment to emphasize that passion all by itself, however essential it may be, *is not enough*, and it is not the only thing that Michael Jordan brought to the table.

We have a saying in my office: "Passion without discipline equals chaos." I really do believe that. The passion half of the equation was the easiest thing to see in Jordan's professional basketball career, but it would have been impossible without the daily discipline or the fanatical commitment to *training* that Jordan also exemplified. Remember, we're talking about somebody who failed to make his varsity basketball team on the first try.

The sales managers I train often ask themselves questions like this:

- What is the difference between a salesperson who has passion and a salesperson who does not have passion?
- Do you think customers pick up on passion?
- How can we instill passion in our sales force?

These are important questions, but they're not the *only* questions we should be asking.

It is impossible to achieve long-term success simply by instilling passion in a sales force. If that were all it took, you could just put on rock-and-roll music in the office and your company's revenues would instantly rise. The passion your people bring to the table must be *matched* by a willingness to look at their own numbers, a willingness to improve in key skill areas, and a willingness to commit to a specific goal by a specific point in time.

The Wrong
Role Model

Now, if we actually had the time to tell people what to do in every situation, and how to do what we want them to do in order to achieve a certain income goal, they'd have a much higher likelihood of success. That is certainly what we would do if we had infinite time for each employee.

We wish we had the time for that. We don't.

As a result, since we don't tend to tell our people that stuff every day, and since they don't have any sense of how long it'll take to do that before they get to where they want to be, an interesting thing starts to happen, especially if we have no one-on-one coaching plan in place for this person. (You're thinking I'm about to tell you that they get frustrated and give up on the job. Right?)

Actually, *before they get so frustrated that they give up on the job,* people start to do something else as a survival technique. They will try this technique even though it often results in acts that seem completely illogical from the manager's point of view, and even though it often means going totally contrary to what their manager may have asked them to do.

Salespeople will copy what 80 percent of the rest of the salespeople do.

That's the "survival strategy."

They look around and say, "Well, what is everybody else doing?" Then they pick up a pattern, and they do that.

This is kind of the inverse of the 80/20 rule. We're used to thinking that the 80/20 rule means that 80 percent of your income comes from 20 percent of your customers. Well, there's a similar pattern at work in the sales force that very few people recognize: that *20 percent of the sales force is really good and 80 percent really isn't.*

The problem comes when a salesperson starts to look around and ask, "Well, what is everyone else doing?" (Again: Why do they start looking around? Because we aren't working with the person every day, as we wish we could.)

If we don't pick a role model for that person, which we usually don't, the salesperson generally picks a role model. That's just the way new salespeople are.

Well, guess what? The person she picks is someone she happens to see around the office. She doesn't pick the person she *doesn't* see around the office. (How could she?)

In most sales organizations, that means the new salespeople are picking one of the *bottom* 80 percent of your organization's performers, rather than the *top* 20 percent. That's because the people who are in the top 20 percent are out closing deals.

So, typically, if you let a salesperson in a field sales environment choose someone to show him the ropes, it's pretty much guaranteed that he's going to choose someone who really isn't the best model of how to succeed at a high level within that organization. You get all the wrong strategies.

We see this guy who's not doing too well and he makes $2 a day, but somehow he keeps showing up day after day after day. Well, the critical thirty-day or sixty-day ramp-up period is going to be reinforced to match this behavior, and the result is a daily sales level of $2 a day.

Or consider this. Another salesperson—maybe one of the top 20 percent—happens to be in the office and has been with this company for ten years and in the business for another twenty before that. But as the new salesperson, I don't know how long she's been in the business. All I know is that when she prospects it looks different than when I prospect. Here's the ten-year veteran prospecting: She's reading the newspaper, drinking coffee, and the phone rings. The veteran picks up the phone. "Hey, Joe! How are you? Thanks for calling. Sure you can come by tomorrow. Great, let me just take that order."

Then the phone rings again. "Hey, Joe! Hey, thanks for calling in. Sure, let me take that order for you."

Apparently, some salespeople get special phones that ring all the time. The inexperienced salesperson is thinking, "Wow! I gotta get one of those phones that rings all the time! My phone *never* rings."

The truth is the new salesperson has to *make somebody else's phone ring*. The experienced salesperson gets all those inbound calls because she has her name out there, she has generated a certain amount of activity, and she has a certain reputation. She's reached a point in her career when she's collecting the dividends from all her hard work; she's now doing a certain amount of business that bounces back more or less automatically, because of the quality of her work and the precision of her prospecting. It's a nice place to be. The problem is, though, that *to imitate the ten-year veteran the way she sells ten years into her job is the wrong thing for the new salesperson to do.*

You know what would be good to know? What was she doing eight or nine years ago? Or even better, what was she doing in her first six weeks on the job?

But if I'm a brand-new salesperson, I can't see that. So, the problem is that people tend to gravitate toward the patterns that they see in the office. Sometimes those are positive; sometimes they're not. Very often people notice patterns that are totally inappropriate for them based on where they're at in their sales career, and maybe even inappropriate for long-term success in the organization as a whole.

The Big Question

So, you have all these challenges as a sales manager. That's what you're up against. And, of course, you don't just have these issues with one person. You have five, ten, fifteen, or twenty people to keep track of.

The job of managing a sales team successfully is considerably more complex than the job of hitting quota. Salespeople are sometimes skeptical about this contention, and therein lies part of the problem: They imagine that motivating a team to hit and exceed sales benchmarks is mostly a matter of sitting back and watching other people do the work, and sometimes there's some resentment toward managers because salespeople really don't understand what we do.

We know, though, how much we have to do, and how little time exists to do it. The job of coaching sales teams has to be done with lots of different people, it has to be done at a high level of quality, and it typically has to be done by managers who are pressed for time.

Let's start at the beginning. When you and I hire the individual members of our sales teams, it stands to reason that we do not hire people whom we believe to be *unqualified* for the job. In other words, we think that the people we hire have the capacity to perform the job of selling what our organization has to offer. If we did not think that, we certainly would not have hired them in the first place. So, anyone who actually makes it on staff did so because someone, somewhere along the line, believed, with good faith, that the applicant has the makings of someone who could sell our stuff.

We also expect that the people we hire have the correct skills to do the job. In other words, not only are they temperamentally suited for the job, but we believe that they have at least some of the basic abilities that a non-salesperson might lack in moving somebody into the status of "customer." Again, if they had no skills for the job in question, we would not hire them.

And finally, having selected the right person, with the right abilities, someone along the line in our organization actually believed that the salespeople who are already on our staff were motivated to do the job. They are ready to take their natural gifts, combine them with the specific skills related to selling our products or service, and they are eager to get to work, close sales, increase the value of the average account, and generally help us to retain or expand market share. Again—if we did not believe that they were willing to do this, we would not have hired them!

A question then arises.

If we have the right people, with the right skills, who are already motivated to do the job, *why don't our teams always hit their goals?* In other words, why is there, typically, a gap between what we expect and what they actually do?

This seems like a simple question, but it takes a lot of experience to answer. I would like to ask you to think it over carefully before you move on to the next chapter. If any given salesperson on your team was considered, at one time or another, to be the right person, with the right skills, and the right motivation, *why would he or she ever fail to meet quota?*

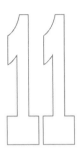

The Answer

The reason salespeople do not actually perform up to our expectations—even though we hire them in the belief that they understand the job, possess the skills for the job, and are motivated to use those skills—is that we, the managers, get it wrong.

We are usually *overly optimistic* about the understanding, skill level, and motivation of people on our sales team.

It is only understandable that we should be optimistic because inspiring a sales team is not the kind of job you can do well by assuming the worst in people. There are plenty of technicians, engineers, quality control specialists, and other professionals whose living depends on the assumption that everything will go wrong. However, I have yet to run into a successful sales manager whose honest opinion of his team was that they were a bunch of idiots who had no meaningful skills and were not inclined to use them.

On the contrary, we usually go out of our way to find reasons to believe that the people we have hired are the right people. And in fact, more often than not, they are the right people. They just do not have the same level of understanding, aptitude, and motivation that we usually assume they do.

To be specific, the reason a team fails even though it is filled with people who *should* be able to perform the job of selling superbly, at least by our standards as managers, is that, in the real world, the vast majority of the people on our team only kind of understand what they are supposed to be doing. That is hard for managers to accept because it means that we have not always done a great job explaining exactly what we want from our sales team. But it is, in fact, the case.

We do not like to admit it, but the fact is that people on our sales team truly do not understand what we expect from them. I'll clarify this point in a few chapters. For now, just take my word for it that, even if you believe you have made yourself absolutely clear on exactly what you expect from your sales staff, there is at least one person who only *kind of* understands what you want in at least one important area.

In addition, we need to admit that a fair number of the salespeople we wish to motivate and inspire to great heights only *kind of* possess the skills necessary to carry out the job of selling at a satisfactory level. It is easy for us to overlook this fact because, as a profession, sales is influenced by personalities. We sometimes hire people based on their personalities, maybe even believing that those personality traits that allowed us to be a successful salesperson will also encourage *this* salesperson to excel. However, very often someone who has a personality style that is quite similar to ours, or to that of someone who sells effectively or has done so, lacks essential knowledge about basic matters such as prospecting, gathering information, and closing the sale.

Finally, as managers, we have to admit that the people who report to us may only be *kind of* motivated to carry out the job with the skills they possess, because we often don't understand what motivates our staff. As a result, we find ourselves working with someone who *kind of* understands what we expect, only *kind of* possesses the skills necessary to give us what we expect, and only *kind of* wants to do so. It is not that surprising that sales teams frequently miss the mark. That missing the mark is reflected in longer-than-necessary sales cycles, missed quotas, and high turnover.

What to do?

The Coaching Model

What to do?

Implement **a proven coaching model.**

Everything that follows is designed to help you *implement* the model that appears on the next page. It is the foundation of this book.

Many salespeople who, we believe, understand what is expected of them may not actually understand precisely what we want. The first and most important part of our job is to get them to understand the role as we envision it. I have devoted an entire section of the book to this. The bottom element of our coaching model, or the foundation, defines the goal and the expectations. If the person does not understand exactly what is expected of him—regardless of whether he is a senior salesperson or somebody we just hired yesterday—then an effective sales manager must *teach that person in an effective way what is expected from a salesperson in this organization.* Another way to say this is that we must first **clarify the salesperson's role.**

Once we move beyond the job of ensuring that the salesperson is on the same page as we are, we have to identify whether he has the ability or skills. This brings us to the second portion of the coaching model, which focuses on our responsibility as managers to **define the skills that are necessary for improvement** and to train the members of our team in those skills.

The third phase of the coaching model focuses simply on whether the person is actually implementing what we have trained him or her to do. It is quite common for people who know how to prospect, for instance, to postpone prospecting. If the person postpones the prospecting for weeks and months on end, there is a potential crisis to deal with. So, in order to **make sure all of the skills are being implemented,** we have to assemble an effective mentoring and coaching program, and that, too, is the focus of an entire section of this book.

You may think that is the end of the process, but there is a fourth element based on recognition. Once someone succeeds for us, it is only common sense, and strategically sound sales management strategy, to **recognize and celebrate sales victories** in front of the group.

When we put our model together, it looks like this:

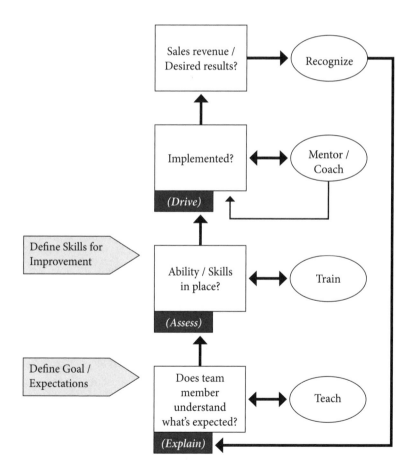

Running for the Horizon?

Let's look at this whole process another way. You've probably seen the pictures of the beginning of the annual New York City Marathon—all those crowds at the starting line, getting ready to start that grueling twenty-six-mile-long course. Here's my question. How many people who *start* a marathon race actually *complete* it?

Ready for a surprise? The answer, as it turns out, is upward of 95 percent. In other words, if you were to monitor a major marathon, like the yearly New York race, and track every one of the hundreds of participants, elite runners, and newcomers to the sport, local and international entrants, you would find that roughly nineteen out of every twenty of those participants complete the twenty-six-mile course.

I was astonished by this statistic. When I was first asked this question, my estimate was that approximately 50 percent of all those who signed up to run the race would actually complete the event. I was way off. Of course, the vast majority of them do not finish anywhere near the actual winners of the race, but they do finish!

Here's my question. What makes a group achievement like that possible?

Before we try to answer that, or understand how this all relates to sales, let me ask you to consider a very different kind of race.

As it happens, the U.S. government sponsors this race. If you were to sign up for the army's elite Delta Force, and if you somehow made it through the initial battery of tests, exclusions, and security double-checks, you would eventually be asked to run this truly remarkable footrace.

You would be gathered with everyone in your unit and given the following instruction: *Run until you can't run anymore!*

You read right. Part of the training for entry into this elite military unit is a race that has a beginning point but, seemingly, no ending point. The participants are told to run until they simply cannot run any farther. They are not given a specific distance. To the contrary, they are given no measurable goal whatsoever. They simply are supposed to run until they collapse.

Eventually, someone steps in and tells anyone who is still upright that it is time to stop. But guess the number of people out of a hundred who actually are still left running around the track by the time the officers in charge intervene.

What was your guess?

If it was anything like mine, it was high. Roughly 98 percent of the group *drops out.*

In other words, it is just about exactly the opposite of the New York Marathon scenario. Ninety-eight out of one-hundred participants fail to complete the event. He or she simply concludes that the limits of physical endurance have been reached. Only 2 percent keep running until the officers tell them to stop.

Here's the punch line: The officers usually intervene *well before anyone has run 26 miles.*

So, look at all the pieces of the puzzle. The people who run the New York Marathon know about how far away the finish line is, and 95 percent of them run twenty-six miles. People in the Delta Force race don't have any idea how far away the finish line is, and 98 percent of them don't come close to running twenty-six miles.

Now, what does this tell us about sales? Well, these two examples suggest that managers have a particularly important role in determining whether someone is going to burn out. Unless you are simply trying to identify the most hardened bodies and souls, so that you can take them into hand-to-hand combat, you will probably want to establish a system under which people are *more* likely to cross the finish line, rather than *less* likely.

Yet, the vast majority of sales managers in the United States today operate under what I call an "unwitting Delta Force" mindset. In other words, they set seemingly impossible goals—not because they want to identify high achievers, but because they simply do not have the imagination or intelligence to identify any other kind of goal.

If you set a sales goal for someone such as, "You have to do better this quarter," or "You have to close more sales," you are dramatically contributing to the likelihood that that person is going to feel high levels of stress and eventually drop out of your team.

The goal that says, "You just have to do better," is, like the "run until you can't run any more" goal, *impossible to benchmark.*

Think about it. A salesperson never knows when this kind of goal has been achieved. There is nothing to measure. There's no way for someone to get a sense of when he or she has reached the quarter point, when the halfway point has been attained, or when the finish line is in sight.

Now consider the manager who says something like this: "Bill, I need you to make ten more dials every day. That's fifty more dials a week. Considering your current ratios, that's two more first appointments a week, and I think that's what you need to hit your quota for closed sales this month."

This kind of goal is analogous to the goal that a participant sets before the beginning of the New York Marathon. ("I'm just starting out . . . I'm a quarter of the way there . . . I'm halfway home. . . .")

For someone who is currently making only five dials a day, ten more dials may be an ambitious goal (at first), but it is, nevertheless, measurable. If managers set goals like this, their salespeople will always know how close they are to attaining the goal at any given moment. If they receive encouragement and support along the way, they will know when they are getting ready to cross the finish line. And they'll be much less likely to fall by the wayside.

If you want a sales team that sticks around, a sales team that buys into goals they understand, a sales team that runs a challenging course for you all the way—make sure you are giving them New York Marathon–type goals that they can measure. Stay away from the "run until you can't run any more" goals that they can't measure.

The Swimmer

One of our salespeople used to be a competitive swimmer; he swam competitively for eleven years.

If you do anything for a very long time, you will discover that sometimes you win and sometimes you lose. There may be a hundred people or more in a particular race. One way to look at it is that the winner is really the person who did his personal best. Another way to look at this, of course, is that the person who finished one-fiftieth of a second ahead of the person who came in second is the winner. Maybe both kinds of winning are valid, but the second kind gets a lot more notice.

The whole thing about swimming as a sport is that it is a race against exhaustion. It is different from most other sports in that regard. A few other sports are based on exhaustion, the marathon race we just discussed or rugby, but with swimming, when you condition yourself, you really are finding the edge of your own personal exhaustion.

Every coach my salesperson had as a competitive swimmer told him the same thing: In order to get faster, you have to work your way all the way to the point of exhaustion, and experience increasingly intense levels of pain in order to make any progress.

In other words, if you don't work up to the highest threshold of pain, you cannot expect to improve very much. That is the nature of the sport. Well, getting yourself to that level of pain is something the coach cannot do for you. That's something that the swimmer brings to the gate.

And so many swimmers quit, because it is impossible (at least for them) to make the kind of adjustment that requires moving past the very highest level of physical pain. They just can never get themselves to work out consistently to that level.

You do get a group of swimmers who are willing to work as hard as necessary to get to the point of pain and agony, but then they become, almost ironically, inefficient.

Inefficiency in swimming makes it even harder to make any real progress. For example, there is a certain prescribed way to put your arm in the water, to stroke through, and to bring your arm over the top of your head; this stroke has a specific sequence. If you do it exactly right, and you expend the least amount of energy, you will have the greatest pull and the stroke will advance your body efficiently through the water.

But when you get tired, you cheat a little bit and skip a couple of seemingly insignificant steps. For example, look at doing pushups. They are supposed to be done with your back straight; if you arch your back instead, you may do a few more, but it is not as good for you, it is not as efficient, and you do not get as much out of the exercise. So when you become an inefficient swimmer, it *looks* as though you are completing the task at hand, but in fact you are getting less benefit from the exercise.

So—what do the best coaches do? Well, the best coaches are able to get the swimmers who brought themselves to this level of pain and exhaustion and help them maintain, increase, and improve their *efficiency*, at that level. It's a tough assignment for the swimmer, but that's what these coaches do.

Is the swimmer who wins the race the person who "wants to win" most?

Well, everybody wants to win. The key to determining who is going to win any race is not to ask who wants to win while they are standing at the starting line. The key is who is willing to prepare. If all the people were equally willing to prepare for a swimming meet, and they all had been coached to the point where they could perform at a high level, even under the most exhausting conditions, who would come in first?

I don't think it would necessarily be the most efficient person. I think the person who wins would be the one who combines energy, efficiency, *and* the desire to win. If you bring your own sense of drive, you learn all the strategic approaches to improving your efficiency as a swimmer, and if you have a truly superior drive to win—then my guess is you stand a very good chance of coming in first.

If you think of these three things—energy, desire, and efficiency—as being on a curve, and then you figure in people's ability to maintain those levels, you'll find that for every single swimmer one of those three will drop off on occasion.

The good coaches figure out *which element is diminishing*. Is the energy dropping off? Is the desire to win dropping off? Is the swimmer maintaining efficiency as she moves through the water, is she taking some kind of shortcut?

The very best coaches *anticipate* the problem before it is a problem. A great coach knows what to say to each athlete to get him or her to improve at the right time in one of those three specific areas: energy, efficiency, or desire to win.

The Lesson

What's the lesson we should draw from that example of the swimming coach? What we say to our salespeople affects their performance; and what's more, the way we say it and the time we choose to say it can make a huge impact on the performance level that we get from the people who are reporting to us.

Think of it this way. On any given job, success could mean:

- Being the best
- Being better than you've ever been
- Winning an award
- (Fill in the blank)

However you define success, the path to success is always the same. You start off, and you're given a role. *If* you happen to buy into that role, the question becomes, do you have the *skills*, the ability, to achieve the goal you set for yourself within that role? After that, the next question is, are you *implementing* the skills you have?

In sales, just as in swimming, you're often brought onto the team with some level of skills. You may be hired because of certain skills, or you may possess skills that the company decides to supplement with training or with exposure to mentors. But if you (a) understand the role and buy into it, and then (b) actually have the skill, you're off to the races. You can (c) implement.

What most salespeople bring to their basic understanding of what they do for a living is analogous to, let's say, someone who shows up at the gym knowing *roughly* what it is that a boxer does, but not yet possessing the actual skills necessary to go ten rounds or the desire to win necessary to implement those skills and secure a victory in the ring.

Change and the Transition Curve

We want to help our salespeople move from "kind of" understanding the role of the salesperson to *truly* understanding that role.

We want to help them move from "kind of" having the skills necessary to succeed in that role to *actually* possessing those skills.

We want to help them move from being "kind of" motivated to implement those skills consistently to *actually* implementing those skills, day in and day out.

Translation: We're talking about change. Have you ever noticed that some people keep doing things in an old, inefficient way, even though they "know" there's a better way of approaching the task in question? Why don't they change instantly? It would seem logical to change right away, wouldn't it?

In order for a manager, trainer, or anyone else to facilitate constructive change for a given individual, that person has to know where people are to begin with. Simply demanding that your team member, prospect, or colleague "do it the new way" will often make the situation worse.

Here's why. Change happens in certain predictable stages. Any time human beings are challenged to develop a brand-new skill set, we are unlikely to adopt it instantly. To the contrary, we are likely to go through a developmental process with five distinct mindsets.

Mindset #1: Immobilization

We simply don't know what to do—and are frozen in place. Typically, in this mindset, we say things like, "I don't believe in doing x. It just doesn't work for me." We don't even address the issue of whether change is in order. When dealing with people who are at this stage, it's a good idea to begin discussions with questions they will not perceive as threatening or attacking: "Why do you say that?" "What makes you feel that way?" When we're in this mindset, we need *support* from other people.

Mindset #2: Denial (False Competence)

We actively deny that any new approach is necessary. We try to improvise our way "around" the problem, or pretend we have skills that we don't. Typically, in this mindset, we say things like, "It sounds interesting, but the way I'm doing it now works for me." When dealing with people who are at this stage, it's a good idea to begin discussions with them by analyzing what their current activities will actually deliver if they keep doing what they're doing. When we're in this mindset, we need *evidence* that it's time to make a change.

Mindset #3: Incompetence

We encounter serious problems in the absence of the skill. Typically, in this mindset, we say things like, "Yikes—I'm not going to be able to hit so-and-so goal in time." When dealing with people who are at this stage, it's a good idea to begin discussions with an evaluation of what the most important goal is and look at all the options that will get us from point A to point B in the timeframe we require. When we're in this mindset, we need help *identifying the alternatives* available to us.

Mindset #4: Acceptance

Finally convinced that a new way is necessary, we admit that we have a lot to learn and start from scratch. At least we're attempting to develop new abilities! Typically, in this mindset, we ask for help: "Can you show me how you . . . ?" Obviously, the best strategy here for managers is to make sure the person gets the help he or she needs. When we're in this mindset, and not before, we're *ready* to try out new ways of doing things.

Mindset #5: Testing New Behaviors

We explore the limits of the skills we are now actively developing. Typically, in this mindset, we say things like, "I think I'm getting the hang of it." At this point, managers and trainers should celebrate any success—no matter how small—and minimize the long-term importance of any failure. When we're in this mindset, *we're hungry for reinforcement!*

Change, Continued: The Five Stages of the Sales Career

Let's continue our discussion of change in the professional selling environment. There are five stages to the sales career, five periods of professional change and growth that apply specifically to the sales professional. If you manage people who sell for a living, you should know what these five stages are!

Stage One: The Novice

The Novice relies heavily on other team members; he or she is still in the "learning the ropes" phase. The Novice may place too much importance on a single prospect and neglect the importance of effective prospect management.

Stage Two: The Contributor

The Contributor works more autonomously than the Novice and can anticipate prospect expectations and manage the sales cycle more effectively. Contributors tend to be strongly goal oriented and to show a great deal of commitment to their work. They need less help than Novices when it comes to managing their own time, gathering the unique prospect information necessary to develop the right "proposal," and closing the sale. A common challenge is an unwillingness to reach out to other team members for help in securing larger and more complex deals.

Stage Three: The Performer

The Performer serves as a role model for others in the sales organization and assists in the completion of large and complex sales. Performers tend to have a deep experience base and superior people skills. They support and motivate other team members in support of their key goals. These are usually the supreme "team players." Some (but by no means all) performers may become impatient with less experienced colleagues.

Stage Four: The Leader

The Leader chooses to assume a coordinating role in the sales team's activities; he or she is also comfortable developing and supporting new talent. Leaders can articulate the company vision and support key partnerships that arise within the sales team. Effective Leaders know how to win group support for new and challenging goals established by the higher-ups in the organization. Many Leaders find that balancing work and personal spheres can be a challenge.

Stage Five: The Builder

The Builder channels his or her entire personality into the mission of building the company, often at the expense of family ties. Builders are so committed to the long-term success of the group that they are often compared to people with religious callings or vocations. It is a matter of faith to them that the company overcome competitive and market challenges, grow, and prosper in the long term. Most chief executives and presidents—still very much salespeople regardless of their title—are Builders in the final phase of a stellar sales career. Whatever their job title, these salespeople tend to have superior executive, team-building, and long-term strategic abilities. Their own high standards and extraordinary commitment are other important assets. A common challenge area for the Builder is that others may perceive him or her as eccentric, paradoxical, or even autocratic.

Those are the five stages. You need not move all the way forward to the Builder stage to experience a satisfying career, but you should be able to identify where you are—and where you want to be—within this model.

Trying to perform at one level before mastering the proficiencies and over-coming the challenges of the previous level leads to "stage uncertainty." This kind of uncertainty is a primary source of burnout-inducing stress for sales professionals.

Seniority in selling is not to be confused with ability.

Sales careers move forward—or stagnate. When they don't move forward, the people attached to them may accumulate seniority *without improving their sales skills or ability to contribute*. When sales careers do move forward, people tend to follow the pattern outlined here.

Note that people can (and many do) remain in one of the first three categories for years. The mere fact that someone has been on the job for a substantial period is not an indicator that the salesperson is learning more, achieving more, or contributing more to the organization than in the past.

When salespeople commit to continuous growth and achievement over time, and when they consistently take actions that expand their capacities, they eventually make progress toward the latter stages of the sales career, which are analogous to those of the successful entrepreneur or seasoned executive.

You can have a salesperson who is young and inexperienced, and the good news is he is very coachable, but the bad news is he really does not know what to do, and he needs to have his hand held. You can hold his hand, but the bad news may be that you have to in order to get any kind of results. At the other extreme, you have a salesperson who not only does not need any handholding, but is so independent that you cannot hold his hand even if you want to. You may say you want a salesperson who can do the job all by himself right out of the box. Yet, all too often, that same person can be a challenge to manage.

What We Figured Out in This Section

Let's step back and look at what we have covered so far.

- We learned that three very different skills are required for skills success, namely *energy, selling skills,* and *value retention skills.*

- We learned that passion without discipline equals chaos.

- We know that the salespeople we hired in the belief that they understood what the job was actually may only *kind of* understand what the job is.

- We know that the salespeople we believed to possess certain skills, such as prospecting or running a meeting, may actually only *kind of* possess those skills.

- We learned that the salespeople we believed to be implementing everything they knew about selling actually might only be *kind of* implementing what they know.

- These mismatches are, in all likelihood, why they are not hitting quota.

- We learned that some salespeople give up right at the point when they are about to make money with us, and that there are a variety of reasons for this, including the following:
  - The goal we give them may not be clear enough.
  - They may not be sure what is actually necessary to achieve the goal.

- They may have peer pressure issues.
- They may have problems about the way our products or services are perceived.
- They may have no clear sense about how long it is likely to take to attain their financial and social goals by working for us.

- We learned that the coaching model—which focuses on confirming the right role (expectations), confirming the actual skill levels and training as necessary, and working with the salesperson to ensure that he or she is motivated to implement the skills—culminates in a recognition or reward for the salesperson.

- We learned that salespeople approach change on the job through a series of five different mindsets, and that only the last of these mindsets requires testing personal limits and instilling creativity.

- We learned that there are five stages to the sales career: the Performer, the Leader, the Builder, the Novice, and the Contributor.

These then, are what I consider the basics, the elements a manager needs to know before attempting to implement what follows in this book. As you can imagine, a great deal of your success or failure in this undertaking will depend on how you understand the job of the sales coach. Before we move on to the next section of the book, though, I want to share my definition of effective coaching:

Effective coaching means achieving team success by getting your team to perform your view of their roles.

Let's look at strategies for doing that.

Do They Understand Their Roles?

Every person on your staff contains an unlit candle.
Your job as a manager is to set the environment so that they
themselves can light that candle. Identifying what the salesperson's role
really is, and making sure the salesperson truly understands that role,
is like striking the match and handing it to the salesperson.
They can't light the candle before striking the match.

The Role
Discrepancy
Exercise

When I deliver a coaching program in person, I generally begin the day by reviewing the managerial basics you read about in Part I. I then ask the participants to take part in the following exercise, which is, I think, perhaps the most important activity of the entire program.

It's called a **Role Discrepancy Exercise**, and it helps managers and salespeople alike to get a fix on how widely their perceptions of each other's roles can vary.

The exercise is simple. To start with, you don't even need to think of a specific salesperson, although I recommend that you eventually expand the exercise and perform it in conjunction with every salesperson on your team. For now, though, all you have to do is fill in each of the four columns you see in the following table.

Role Discrepancy Exercise

Team member's view of team member's role	Manager's view of team member's role	Team member's view of manager's role	Manager's view of manager's role

Notice that the first column asks you to write down a few thoughts on how your salesperson views his or her role in the company. (It usually does not take very much imagination on the manager's part to generate four or five sentences of sufficient accuracy here.) The second column asks you to identify the manager's view of that same salesperson's role. The third column is where the salesperson writes down his or her view of the manager's role. The fourth column is where you look at your view of your own role in the company.

Take a few moments now and write down bullet points for *each* of these categories on a separate sheet of paper. Try to list at least six items under each heading.

It's no joke—you really do need to complete this exercise before you can get anything meaningful out of the rest of this book. Please jot down some bullet points under each of the four columns before proceeding to the next chapter.

How Salespeople View Their Jobs

When we ask sales managers to think like salespeople and answer the question, "What do salespeople in your company think their role is?" we get some interesting answers. Here are some of the things that they say:

- Sell.

- Close effectively.

- Find prospects.

- Maintain relationships with existing customers.

- Perform certain administrative tasks.

- Forecast.

- Get to work on time.

- Get expenses in.

But if you ask the same group of managers to list what *managers* think the salesperson's role is, you'll usually see these two elements on the list.

- Make quota.

Or, even better:

- Exceed quota.

Then I say, "You see that you wrote 'Meet or exceed quota'?' Did you notice that doesn't even show up on the salesperson's list?"

All too often, in the real world, that element is not on the salesperson's list either. In fact, *most* salespeople I have worked with over the years tend not to think in terms of hitting or meeting a quota. They usually see their job as having more to do with surviving from month to month and quarter to quarter.

A manager would quickly point out that goal certainly *involves* quota, but the actual goal of hitting or exceeding quota usually is not something that salespeople want to think about or be held accountable for. If you leave them to their own devices, they won't describe it as part of their job description. They just don't view their role as encompassing making or surpassing quota, even though that is typically the most important thing for any manager who supervises them.

Well, if salespeople do not think hitting quota or beating quota is part of their job, there is going to be a discrepancy. As sales managers, we constantly have to reinforce and work with the team to help them remember that a very important part of their job is hitting or exceeding quota.

We cannot assume that because we once mentioned quota at the beginning of the month or the beginning of the quarter, salespeople will see meeting or beating quota as an integral part of their job. They won't.

Even if we mention it every week, we may find that it *still* slips off the radar screen. We have to find a way to work on quotas, not merely on an individual level but on the group level. We have to talk (obsessively!) about group quotas *and* individual quotas, just for salespeople to remember that they're part of the job description. We have to reinforce the importance of team quota numbers with the group as a whole, and we have to reinforce (in private meetings) the importance of what activities support (or don't support) hitting individual quotas.

When there is a discrepancy between what the manager thinks should be number one on the person's priority list and what the salesperson thinks should even appear on the priority list, *we can't count on the salesperson doing the reinforcement that will change the way he or she views the role.* We, the managers, have to take responsibility for that reinforcement. Otherwise, the person's conception of his or her role will stay the same.

110 Things vs. Two Things

A few years ago, one of our clients counted all of the things we teach. It turns out that, in our appointment–making training program for salespeople, we cover no fewer than 110 different topics related to the appointment-making process.

So, a client will hire us to train those 110 or so things for salespeople who work for them—people they think would benefit from hearing our 110 topics on appointment making. The salespeople are in the training program *because* they are supposed to hear 110 things. We are there to teach them those 110 things. And invariably, at the end of the class, somebody from the group will come up and say, "Steve, that was great! I learned two very important things today."

To be polite, I say, "Thank you."

But as they are leaving, I'm thinking, "Gee, you weren't supposed to learn *two* things; you were supposed to learn 110 things!"

Why did they only learn two things? The cynic will say, "Maybe they already knew the other 108 things." Well, the odds are not very good for that being true.

The more realistic explanation is that while we may have covered, say, ten critical points about lead generation, the salespeople believed that providing leads is the manager's job; therefore, at that section of the program, what we had to say was (in their view) irrelevant to their world.

That's a sobering thought if you're a manager who really does want the team to do more lead generation.

Similarly, in our selling skills course, salespeople may disengage and not accept as vitally important all the advice we give on certain topics—say, on building their own managers into their follow-through meetings with prospects. Why? Because they are under the impression "that's not the way we do it here," even though the managers may have requested that they *start* doing it that way.

The problem is that salespeople's *perceptions* of what matches their goals will have a determining influence on how much priority they give new pieces of information from trainers and managers. That's why the Role Discrepancy Exercise is such an important part of the coaching process.

There is often a fundamental disconnect between the reason the salesperson imagines he or she is learning the material, and what the manager would like to emphasize. We have to watch out for any single element of the job description *we* have in mind at which the salesperson throws up his or her hands and says (or even thinks), "Hey, that's not my job!" That is where we may have to look more closely at how the role is being interpreted on both sides.

If what we are trying to get them to improve in does not overlap with their own conception of what the job is, then they are never really going to "get it." They will not pay attention to information that they believe, for whatever reason, is irrelevant to their world.

"Hey, I'm Doing *My* Job!"

Managers think (for instance) that the salesperson's job is all about exceeding quota, and then they get upset because most salespeople do not do that.

Managers wonder why salespeople simply don't get out and do it, but they may not recognize that the salesperson views his job as simply to sell. And that is, after all, something that the salesperson is doing!

You really can sell and not make quota. So the salesperson is thinking, "What are you worried about? I'm selling, aren't I?"

Or, in other words, "Hey, I'm doing *my* job!"

What other topics do managers think should be high on the salesperson's list of role responsibilities but somehow do not make it on to the salesperson's radar screen?

Here's a big one: *forecast accurately*. That is a common answer. Note how it differs from what's on the salesperson's list. The salesperson writes down the word *forecast* on the list of role responsibilities, but the manager writes: "forecast *accurately*."

Isn't there a difference between forecasting and forecasting accurately? Of course! Anybody can forecast. But forecasting *accurately* is something that salespeople often do not feel motivated to do. They will give what they call their "best guess," of course, but if quarter after quarter after quarter there is no real correlation between the "best guess" and actual performance, salespeople tend not to worry about it that much. For sales managers, however, this disconnect can be a real nightmare.

This is not to say that forecasting is easy. As a weather forecaster on TV once said, "It's very difficult to accurately predict weather that hasn't happened yet." That's the trick, isn't it?

As if to explain this seemingly obvious point to people like me, the meteorologist continued: "It would be difficult to forecast that it's actually going to rain in New York if the rain clouds haven't yet formed over Chicago, which would be the normal path."

Similarly, if the sale is not even yet in its formative stages, then how can we forecast when or if it is going to happen? Alternatively, if the sale were no longer in its formative stages, how would we predict when it was going to finish? We would have to be comfortable and familiar with our process and *know how long* it usually takes us to move from point A to point B in order to get meaningful information.

There is a difference between what the salesperson says is part of his role—to generate a forecast—and what the manager expects—to generate an *accurate* forecast.

"I thought you just wanted me to put any old numbers together."

"No, actually I'm interested in what's *really going to happen* thirty days from now."

"Ah, I see. . . . Well, let me think about that."

Guess what? If they work together, and actually communicate on a regular basis, they can generate meaningful numbers, by examining how far each cloud system (read: potential deal) has progressed. The sales manager's experience about the nature of the deal, the likelihood of closure, and the potential value of the deal should all come into play. (For more on accurate forecasting, see Chapter 52. For a much more detailed discussion of forecasting, see my book *Getting to "Closed".*)

In what other areas do sales managers and salespeople differ when it comes to the salesperson's role? Here is one of the most common: *Keep good records day to day.*

Typically, a manager expects keeping accurate records to be second nature for a salesperson. Unfortunately, this item usually does not even show up on the salesperson's list! Some managers think, "Gosh, even though I've put them through a whole training course on how to update things in the database, they're not using that information. What do I have to do?" Guess what? They never really bought into the role. You need to connect on that first, *before* you try to train them on the software or anything else related to recordkeeping.

We could probably list many other examples of disconnects, but you can see the pattern here. Mismatches between the salesperson's understanding of what the role is and the manager's understanding of what the role is really can be an obstacle to any kind of substantial or measurable performance increase.

Now let's move on to the manager's role.

The Manager's Role

What does a salesperson think the manager's role ought to look like?

This is a little bit like asking what a child or a teenager thinks the parent's role is. Salespeople often give answers like:

- Bust my hump./Make my life difficult. (This one actually comes up quite a lot. I wonder if salespeople seriously believe that a company would hire someone simply to irritate someone else in the organization.)

- Be a buffer between the salesperson and upper management.

- Help me close deals.

This last one is an excellent idea—as long as the sales manager knows what's going on in the sale, has enough information, and agrees that this should be part of the role.

Here's what usually happens. You're working with a sales representative, and, let's be honest, you don't spend quite as much quality time with the salesperson as you wish you could. So, you finally have a day or a half a day to spend with her. You're driving around, talking about all kinds of things, trying to catch up with the person, and it really isn't until the car goes into the parking lot for the next appointment that you start talking about that particular meeting. So you're getting out of the car, and you ask the salesperson to tell you what's going to happen at this meeting. As the salesperson gets out of the car, she says to you, "Well, the last time I met with this customer, he wanted a fifty-percent discount, so I told him I'd bring in my boss."

Good luck!

If that is the kind of deal a sales manager is supposed to "help close," it is not much fun as a job. Superman could not close a deal like that. (By the way, I'll share more on this important subject of how managers can work with salespeople in the next three chapters.)

Okay, here are some other items that appear on this list:

- Make sure I get paid.

- Train me.

- Know when to be there for me.

- Know when to give me space.

Salespeople often say, for example, "I don't want to be micromanaged, but I don't want you to be off in the distance either. I need you to be just there at the exact moment when I need help, but not at any other time."

It takes quite a manager to fill that job description.

The real point is that during all of these sessions, both when the managers play the salespeople and when the salespeople fill out the exercise for themselves, the salespeople come away with the impression that the only real function the manager has is to coach them. Managers have no other job as far as salespeople are concerned; but, in fact, if you ask a manager what his or her real job is, you get a variety of answers, including:

- Hiring.

- Firing.

- Coaching.

- Assessing members of the sales team.

- Developing accurate forecasts.

- Performing administrative work.

- Working to retain important customers by keeping them happy.

- Making suggestions to marketing department.

- Making suggestions to product development people.

The fact is, coaching will never be 100 percent of this job. The issue is not how to make coaching 100 percent of the job, but rather: Is there any way we can work together to build the 5 percent of our time we are spending on coaching into 10 or 15 percent of the time? If it is only going to be 5 percent of our time, how do we make that 5 percent more effective?

You don't have time for miscommunication about what the role is. You need to work this out, face-to-face, with your salesperson—not in a threatening way, but as a starting point, so you can do the rest of the coaching job properly in the limited time you have. If you don't do the Role Discrepancy Exercise with *each* of your salespeople, and discuss the results one-on-one, the resulting communication problems can block anything else important from happening in your coaching with your people.

Now, just as there are things that *we* believe salespeople should understand about their role that they sometimes ignore, there are also things they want us to do that we overlook. As we've seen in this chapter, one element of the sales manager's job that is very rarely listed by sales managers but that has a way of showing up consistently in this Role Discrepancy Exercise is serving as a "senior salesperson" at key moments in the sales process. In other words, helping salespeople close deals.

If you did not include this item on your list of responsibilities, I would like to encourage you to think about taking on at least some responsibilities in this area. To find out why this is so important, and to get some ideas about how to do it despite the fact that your schedule is jammed, please read the next chapter.

Your Role as "Senior Salesperson"

Sometimes when I suggest to sales managers that they have an opportunity, and perhaps a responsibility, to be involved in the sales process of their salespeople, I get skeptical looks and responses.

The idea really is not as far-fetched as it may seem. You are judged by the success or failure of the people who report to you, and you possess, in virtually all areas, significantly more expertise than the salespeople whom you are hoping to coach. (It's possible, of course, that you may possess less expertise than some extremely accomplished salespeople, but improving the results of those people is typically not the focus of most sales managers.)

In this book I am trying to share some strategies for improving the results of those team members whose outcomes you really can help to improve—for example, by getting out there and helping them close the sale. If this seems like a breach of authority or a breach of your job description, or a waste of your time, let me assure you that it is not. In the animal kingdom, many species can only learn to catch food when taught by a parent. Whether we like it or not, human beings are one of those species. Of course, evolution has changed the ultimate goal a bit; in place of food, human beings often find themselves in pursuit of commission checks. We may approve of or disapprove of the fact that the sales manager has had to adopt this parental role, but the reality is that people learn by doing, and they typically only learn by doing once they have seen someone else accomplish the task.

Instead of simply lecturing your people, get in there and help them close a deal or two. How? Here are some ideas on how you can do exactly that.

First, embrace a selling philosophy that is based on the idea of "getting to the Next Step."

"Getting to the Next Step" really means *finding out whether the customer will agree to a scheduled meeting or discussion that I, the salesperson, believe is necessary to eventually close the sale, and to do it within my average sales cycle.* (Warning: I *will* be repeating this.)

It's a mouthful, I know, but that really is the full-scale explanation of "getting to the Next Step," and it's worth emphasizing in your dual role as manager and senior salesperson.

Why You Should Do This

There's a compelling reason for you to step in occasionally to the salesperson's selling process:

All too often, salespeople do not bother to identify what has to happen next for the deal to close.

On the other hand, anyone who has been managing a sales team for more than, say, three or four months, learns to focus obsessively on this very issue. Let me give you one example. It has to do with price.

I am a firm believer that some kind of reference to the price of the product should come up during the first meeting or discussion with a prospect, and I believe most experienced sales mangers would agree. In fact, a fair number of the highly successful salespeople I have coached over the years make a point of raising price issues *over the phone, while attempting to set the first appointment.* I am not necessarily advocating that your people do that, because covering price over the phone requires very strong bonding and rapport skills. I am suggesting that some kind of discussion about pricing ranges needs to take place at the first meeting, so that the salesperson and the prospect can make an intelligent, informed decision about whether it makes sense to have a second meeting.

Now, as it turns out, sales managers tend to be very, very good at this. Salespeople as a group, and specifically inexperienced salespeople who are relatively new at the job, tend to be very bad at it.

The salespeople who are bad at this either don't raise the issue of price at all during the first meeting, or offer a price "range" that is so broad as to be totally meaningless as an indicator of this prospect's seriousness in moving forward. To give an example, salespeople might say something such as, "This program ranges in price, and might cost you anywhere between $100 and $250,000 depending on the specifics." What kind of meaningful information does that give the prospect?

An experienced sales manager, on the other hand, will make a point of referencing a meaningful price range that actually reflects "about what we are looking at." Managers will usually do this in such a way as to leave themselves room to maneuver on pricing, while still making it clear, early on, exactly what is going to be necessary to move the relationship forward. After all, the sales manager wants to know if this prospect is capable of writing a check or getting it written!

The sales manager also wants to know whether the decision-maker has the relevant authority to authorize such an expense.

There are a number of ways to raise the issue, including:

- After shaking hands while the prospect is walking with us to the front door of the building: "Just between you and me, I am thinking that this program is probably going to cost you something in the neighborhood of $700 to $1,000 per person. I am a little concerned because I am not sure if that is going to be a problem or not—what do you think?"

- "Before we get started, I wanted to let you know that for people in your industry, this program typically runs between $700 and $1,000 per person. Is that going to be a problem?"

- "I am not sure how we are going to end up pricing this, but the last program I worked on that looked like this, and was in your industry, ended up costing somewhere between $700 and $1,000 per participant. Is that about the price range you were considering?"

- "I'm a little concerned about the price. We typically charge between $700 and $1,000 per participant. " (Stop talking.)

Raising this issue early in the sales cycle does not "alienate the prospect," which is the reason salespeople give for not talking about price in meaningful terms during the first meeting. On the contrary, raising these issues is an excellent way to give the prospect a clear idea of exactly what is happening. If the price is going to be a problem, the sales manager wants to know about it right now. An inexperienced salesperson, on the other hand, not only does not want to know about it right now but may even believe he or she is going to be "in trouble" if it turns out that the meeting with the prospect is not going to advance to the second step.

The moral of the story is that a sales manager is much more likely to know when a second meeting is not warranted and is also likely to be better at identifying obstacles in the pricing structure that will preclude a signed contract.

This is only one of the many ways that you can reduce "the learning curve" of your junior-level people, and I encourage you to do it. Go on a couple of meetings with them, and show them exactly how a pro figures out whether it makes sense to move forward.

Other Ways You Can Help

In addition, you might consider:

- Calling a contact the salesperson tells you is a "great prospect," and leaving a message that says, "I understand it looks as if we are likely to be working together, and I am certainly looking forward to helping make that happen."

  (By the way, this is a truly remarkable sales forecasting tool. If there really is a deal here, you will find out about it soon enough. If there is an obstacle, the contact will immediately call you and tell you in some depth exactly what it is . . . and often will reveal details he or she would not have shared with the salesperson.)

- Rescuing "lost" deals by calling the contact and leaving a message that says, in essence, "I understand that you initially had a good meeting with Jim Smith, our sales representative, and that things went wrong. I am just calling to find out what the problem was, and to apologize on Jim's behalf."

- Another approach is to simply leave a message saying, "I am calling regarding Jim Smith," and to leave your company affiliation and phone number. This technique virtually always receives a return call, at which point you can explain that you are not certain how things went wrong and you want to figure out where Jim screwed up. Again, you will get much better information than you would if the person were talking to the salesperson directly.

That final strategy is well worth considering. I have used it to turn around roughly 10 percent of all of the deals that we have lost initially at my company. Whenever we put the work in on a proposal, and the decision does not go our way, I make a point of reaching out to the decision-maker directly and asking where the salesperson screwed up and how I can help to fix it.

You might think that salespeople would mind this kind of call, but in fact, once they see how effective it is, they are grateful. After all, you are still paying them the commission after you come in to do the damage control!

What We Figured Out in This Section

In this section of the book, we learned that:

- The Role Discrepancy Exercise helps you and your salespeople identify the expectations associated with the job of selling for your company.

- This exercise also helps you fix potentially disastrous misconceptions that managers and salespeople may have about (1) the salesperson's role and (2) the manager's role.

- You, the manager, should occasionally expand your role so that you can act as a "senior salesperson" and get involved in the sales cycle of the people who report to you.

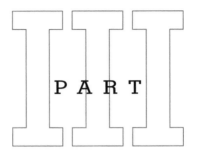

PART

Do They Possess the Skills?

*Twenty-five hundred years ago, Confucius observed that
action was an essential part of all learning. He told his followers,
"I hear and forget. I see and remember. I do and I understand."
What follows is meant to help you help your salespeople understand . . . by doing.*

Headaches

Sales managers have to deal with various headaches from time to time. *Headache category number one* connects to something you will have to work with your human resources people to solve. In this category fall issues like antisocial behavior, mental instability, drug problems, and family issues. Although you can offer support and counseling from another source, there is nothing you can do to fix these problems. Different companies have different guidelines for dealing with these issues, and there's no coaching advice I can give you to help resolve them, because this isn't my field of expertise, and unless you've got a degree in psychology or social work, it isn't yours, either. So admit that, and get help from someone else.

Headache category number two has to do with something sales managers sometimes *try* to coach their way through, and shouldn't. These are what I call "bare minimum" issues.

The headaches in this category arise when the salesperson doesn't even meet the lowest-level professional standards for the job. I call these "no-negotiation" performance areas. Trying to compassionately coach someone through performance issues in these areas is simply unacceptable. It usually backfires with the salesperson in question and sends the wrong message to the rest of the team.

For instance, showing up for work every morning at 9:00 is part of the employment agreement. It is not a negotiable item, and not a subject for coaching discussions. Similarly, if the salesperson is supposed to show up in person for team meetings, there is no sense trying to mount a charm offensive in order to get him or her there. John Smith, your salesperson, needs to show up every week for this meeting. Period. It shouldn't take a United Nations Security Council resolution to get him to materialize, and if it does, you should probably start laying the groundwork that will allow you to get rid of John Smith. (If John Smith is the staff superstar, and you decide to set different rules for him than you set for the rest of the company, you should consider finding a way to let John Smith work from home, so that it will be clear to all and sundry that John has graduated to another level through hard work and close contact with you, the manager.)

Make no mistake. Although there are non-negotiable issues (and only you can figure out what they are and defend them in your work day), *many* areas require discussion and negotiation with your salesperson. The trick is to know which is which. Identify your team's non-negotiable issues early, keep the list short, and repeat it often. Then do your best to listen hard about every item that isn't on that list. (We are constantly telling salespeople that they have to hone their listening skills, but the sad truth of the matter is that we often don't offer a very good example on this front.)

I've found that the majority of sales managers who have a problem in this area tend to be men. I don't know if that makes me a sexist for pointing it out, but it is a fact that I've observed and I, too, am guilty of the syndrome.

One of the most common challenges men have in supervising sales teams falls under the category of what we, in my office, have come to call "male answering syndrome." Often, a salesperson will come to a sales manager with a problem that he or she simply wants to discuss—not necessarily resolve instantly or negotiate, but *discuss*. For a male in charge of a department, however, that can be a very difficult undertaking. I think it's because men are programmed somehow to *solve problems*. So if someone walks into the office and says, "Gosh, I have a terrible headache today," a fair number of men in management positions, particularly in sales management positions, will respond to this by saying something like the following: "You have a headache? Here, take an aspirin."

And then we go back to doing whatever we were doing. The unspoken message is "I solved the problem, please go away."

It's an effective enough strategy for dealing with some issues, but it really doesn't leave much room for human interaction. And sometimes, human interaction is in fact what people need.

So, as a side note, do not fall into the trap of simply "solving" whatever skills-based challenges a salesperson may happen to raise with a curt sentence or two: "Well, you have to make more calls." "That's because you're not opening the meeting right."

One sentence, on such complicated topics, simply isn't going to do the job.

We can, and should, be concise in dismissing attempts salespeople make to ignore our non-negotiable requirements, but we can't assume that means we should be concise about *everything*. There does come a point when a manager has to be willing to invest his or her time in a relationship with the salesperson.

So—we've covered two categories of issues that can give you headaches: a serious personal and/or mental problem, and non-negotiable performance issues. A third group of issues can give you headaches as a manager, and I call the changes we can bring about by effective coaching in this area "skills changes." These kinds of changes are the focus of this section of the book.

Critical Sales Skills

What follows in this section is a brief summary of the critical sales skills that you, as a sales manager, should be prepared to identify and coach your sales team to develop or improve.

If you have already been through one of my training seminars, or if you are familiar with these principles from earlier books, you may be tempted to skip this section, but please don't. I will be addressing some very important issues from the manager's perspective.

> An effective reinforcement campaign will determine the success or failure of your efforts to indoctrinate your people with the principles in this section of the book.

We have a saying around my office: "The secret in the sales training industry is that sales training doesn't work." We say that during our appointments with prospects, and it usually draws a strange look. But the truth is, sales training, *on its own*, really does not work. If you simply spend a day sharing what follows in Chapters 30 through 48 with your sales team, they will get some good information, but they will not actually change their selling habits. To bring about positive change, you can't just deliver a single day "event"—days I like to call "T-shirt events," where the participants all get a special T-shirt for participating. (And nothing else.)

You have to do something more.

So, this part of the book is about the foundational skill concepts. Later on, in Part IV, we'll look at the long-term coaching plan, the follow-through campaign that is central to any meaningful campaign for change.

Your Number-One Competitor

Let me ask you a question. Who would you say is your organization's number-one competitor? When I ask this question during training sessions, I get many different answers, most of them incorrect. I hear people say, our number-one competitor is such-and-such a company, or "Our number-one competitor is our own complacency." These are all very interesting answers but they are not the real answers to the question.

Actually, our real competition is the status quo. The status quo is the force of habit that reflects what our customer is already doing and the way it is now being done.

Whatever that person is doing right now, it is what makes sense to him or her and that is all that really matters in the customer's world.

Believe it. What your sales team's true competition is has nothing to do with any exterior force or new product or service they can buy from somebody else. The true competition is the mental pattern that exists in your prospect's mind, the one that says to him or her, "It makes sense for me to buy x . . ." or even, "It makes sense for me to do nothing. I really prefer not to buy."

The Number-One Prospect

I will often begin a training program by asking the salespeople and managers sitting in front of me to identify the number-one prospect they're working on at that moment.

To me, and to all the people we end up training and to all the people we train, a "prospect" has a specific status. However, it's a status that most salespeople, or at least most salespeople who have not been acquainted with our selling philosophy, routinely ignore. So it's not that surprising that people who offer details to me during training programs about their supposed "number-one prospect" end up telling me things about organizations and people they *wish* they could sell to.

That's not what I'm after when I'm talking about a "prospect." The fact that I *could* sell something to Gargantuan Corporation, the fact that Gargantuan Corporation would definitely benefit from working with my company, the fact that Gargantuan Corporation seems to me to "need" what I offer, or even the fact that Gargantuan Corporation once met with me to discuss the possibility of working with me—all of that is totally irrelevant in our view.

When people say these kinds of things to me during our initial discussion of the "number-one prospect"—"I'm getting ready to call Gargantuan Company back, we had a great meeting six months ago"—I always remove the company from the person's list of prospects.

This is because, in our world, a "prospect" is someone who is *playing ball with me.*

By playing ball with me, I mean the person has demonstrated his or her interest in pursuing the possibility of working with me in a tangible way, namely by scheduling time to meet or to discuss things in depth with me. Typically, that meeting or discussion needs to be on the person's calendar within the next two weeks. If I do not have this tangible evidence of interest from my contact at Gargantuan Corporation, I cannot consider her a prospect. The person is not playing ball with me, no matter how "well" the last discussion may have gone.

The "Great Meeting"

Some years ago, one of my own salespeople came back from a meeting with a prospect we had been pursuing for some time. As soon as the salesperson came back into our office from that meeting, I asked him to take a seat in my office.

"How did the meeting go?" I asked.

"It went great!" the salesperson replied. "The guy asked a lot of questions, he was very interested in our training, he gave me all the right body language signals, and we really established a very firm professional connection. I spent at least two hours in that office, and we reviewed our training programs in more detail than I've ever gone into on a first meeting. The guy was absolutely enthralled, and he was curious about every single one of our training products."

"That's wonderful," I said. "When are you going back?"

"Actually, Steve," the salesperson said, "I'm not going back. We spent so much time on each of the programs, and we did such a thorough analysis of what he was looking for compared to what we offered, that we were able to determine that he really had no use whatsoever for anything on our product list. He asked me never to call him back, ever again."

I'm exaggerating certain elements of the story for emphasis, but I think you see what I'm getting at? So often, salespeople walk into our office with exactly the same story, or at least some variation: The meeting went great. The guy really likes me. The woman in charge of purchasing is precisely our kind of decision-maker. The committee is unhappy with what they have right now. You've heard all that stuff before, and so have I, but at the end of the day, we as managers are obligated to ask the tough question: What is the Next Step?

If there is no commitment to meet or speak with us again, preferably within the next two weeks, then there is no Next Step. And at that point, we as managers are obligated to ask, "Was that *really* a great meeting?"

Four Steps

When I speak to salespeople about the sales process, I usually open the discussion with this question: "If the sales process has four steps, what is the objective of the first step?"

This usually causes a moment of confusion, sometimes because people are used to thinking about the sales process as having more than or fewer than four steps. There are a number of different ways to look at sales. We identify four steps, and once I have assured the group that there's no penalty for thinking about sales in some other way, I restate the question, and ask them to think about what the likely objective or goals of the first step would be.

Inevitably, I hear answers such as, "To get to know the prospect." Or, "To build rapport." Or, "To find out about their needs."

These are all interesting answers, but they are wrong. After I have made my way around the room, I ask the participants one more time to think of the goal of the sales process, and they usually draw a blank, because all of the "rapport-building" and "need identification" answers they have given are the answers they have had drummed into them for the past five or ten or fifteen years by managers and sales trainers.

Then I will explain to them that actually, the goal of the first step in the sales process is simply to *get to the Next Step*. Nothing more, nothing less.

The Next Step

If, as I've said, the goal of the first step of the sales cycle is to get to the Next Step, then the goal of the second step should be pretty clear, as well. It is to get to the third step. And of course, the goal of the third step should be to get to the fourth step.

These answers illustrate an important way of looking at sales. The sales process is dynamic—constantly in motion—it either proceeds relentlessly forward, or ceases to exist.

There is a moment in the classic comedy *Annie Hall*, staring Woody Allen and Diane Keaton, where Allen explains to Keaton that sharks are remarkable animals because they must constantly move in the ocean. If a shark were to be forced to stand still, it would die. He then turns to Keaton and explains that, as far as their relationship is concerned, what they have on their hands is a dead shark.

It is much the same with selling. Either something is moving forward with your prospect, or the prospect does not exist. The people who are "thinking about" committing to some course of action with you are not prospects, no matter how much you might wish that they would work with you. They have made no commitment to any Next Step.

We can get even more specific in our description of *how* we want the process to move forward. I told you that the objective of the first step is always to get to the Next Step, and so on through to the fourth step. When I say, "get to the Next Step," what I mean is this:

"Find out if the customer will agree to a next step that I believe is needed to eventually close the sale—and do it within my average selling cycle."

Sound familiar?

As I mentioned in Part II, we are not going to propose just *any* next step, we are going to focus on the next step that we know, from experience, is likely to move toward an agreement. Some of this experience will come from the salesperson's side and some of it, especially in the early going, is likely to come from the manager's side.

The Sales Process

If we accept that the sales process has four steps, what does the fourth step have to be?

Of course, it is the **close**, which is the point at which the customer agrees to buy from us.

To close the sale, salespeople sometimes resort to lots of different "selling tricks," believing that they can somehow trick the person into agreeing to buy what their company has to offer. Actually, tens of thousands of manipulative selling "tricks" have been committed to paper, and most of them are virtually useless. I say "virtually" because these strategies can in fact deliver sales, but only in situations where the person was going to buy from you anyway.

Here's what I call the "one-third" rule: One-third of all your potential customers will buy from you no matter what you say; one-third of all your potential customers won't buy from you no matter what you say; and one-third of your potential customers *may* buy from you, depending on the skills you bring to the table.

I could give you a long list of the types of tricky selling and closing strategies people have promoted over the years, but it would be a waste of paper. Suffice to say that the next time you hear somebody say something like "Press hard, because you are going to be making three copies," you are in fact being subjected to a manipulative selling trick. I cover the topic of manipulative closing techniques in depth in my book *Closing Techniques (That Really Work!)*.

There is a much better approach to closing the deal, and it has the virtue of simplicity. It sounds like this:

"Makes sense to me. What do you think?"

That, by the way, is my entire closing strategy in a single sentence.

Please note that **we want the prospect to decide to buy; we don't want to have to sell to the prospect.** And that's the whole idea behind this philosophy of selling.

This "makes sense to me" closing strategy is incredibly effective. It either delivers an affirmative answer, in which case you can move forward and start the necessary paperwork to begin working with this person, or, it delivers a negative answer that you can work with. When a prospect tells me, "No, that really doesn't make sense to me, Steve," I do not just sit there dumbfounded nor do I try some tricky response to get the person to change his or her mind. I have a natural question that flows directly and comfortably out of the dialogue:

"Gee, I'm surprised to hear you say that. Most of the people I get to this point of the sale with tell me that it does make sense to go forward. Just out of curiosity, what part of our discussion doesn't make sense?"

At that point, I generally get the information I need to figure out whether this is a potential customer.

What about the Earlier Steps?

In the last chapter, I gave you and your team a reliable closing strategy that sounded like this:

"It makes sense to me. What do you think?"

That is in fact the very best way to close a sale, but guess what? There's a catch.

This closing strategy will only deliver superior results if you deliver a *plan* or *proposal* that is based on some reason that makes sense to this person. And this *proposal* constitutes the third of our four steps.

This is the formal plan, the one that we prepare in support of our eventual question, "Makes sense to me. What do you think?"

Remember, we are looking for a way to change the status quo, to alter what the person has been doing up to this point, whether that is nothing, or whether that is a long-term relationship with somebody else in our industry.

Now, if the closing technique carries a catch, you may have been wondering whether there is a catch associated the proposal step. There is. In our sales philosophy, we can only consider the third step fulfilled if we have generated the *right* proposal for this prospect, the proposal that "makes sense."

So, how do we develop that proposal?

By gathering *information* that focuses on what they are doing now, we can figure out whether we can help them do it better.

> The definition of selling is helping people do what they do
> better.

Think of it this way. How many possible plans, or reasons, could we put together for our prospects? In theory, there are an infinite number.

But of that huge wave of potential proposals, plans, or reasons to buy from us, which is the one we want to present? Obviously, it is the one that "makes sense" to our prospect.

So here is the $64,000 question: How do we figure out which proposal or reason is the one that makes sense to the other person?

The answer is back in the information-gathering stage, which is the second phase of our sales cycle. At this point, we gather as much information about what the person is presently doing as we possibly can. Our questions should be focused—not on what we imagine the other person needs, not on the pain we believe he or she is likely to be experiencing, not on the problems he or she supposedly encounters—on what the prospect is actually *doing* right now.

If we ask about this in terms of the past, the present, and the future and then vary our questioning to include the how and the why, we will, most of the time, get a reasonably accurate view of what this person is actually doing, what is actually taking place in this person's world. That's obvious enough, isn't it?

It is, but we lose sight of the obvious very easily—yet it remains obvious. In fact, I call this whole way of selling "selling to the obvious."

> Sell to the obvious—by asking how and why the person is
> already doing what he or she is doing.

We are going to have a much better chance of identifying the reason, or plan, that needs to go into our proposal, the proposal that will "make sense" to the other person.

Let me give you an example of how this works in our industry, the sales training industry. When I initially meet with somebody, one of my first questions is, "Have you ever thought about doing sales training in the past?"

I will also ask, if the person called me, "Why did you decide to look into sales training?" I might even open the meeting by asking why the person is not working with us right now. In the final analysis, the questions about what the other person is doing—about the status quo—must constitute most of my effort.

I can break down my questioning efforts into this matrix.

Past	
	How?
Present	
	Why?
Future	

The how and the why are particularly important because they often represent my only real strategy for identifying whether the person is capable of getting this decision made for me. Someone who has the decision-making authority knows how that authority was exercised in similar decisions. If I am ever in a situation where I am not certain whether the person I am talking to has the authority to move forward, I will always ask a "how" or "why" question, for example:

"How did you decide on your last sales training vendor? What made you decide to go with that company?"

If the person has absolutely no idea what the process was for selecting the last outside sales trainer, I know that he or she cannot get the decision made for me this time around. It is at that point that I am going to try to incorporate the other people in the organization who do know how this decision was made, and I am going to keep asking that question until I get some kind of access to them. (Tactfully, of course.)

Ask the "how" and the "why," and the "who" will emerge.

There is a lot more to be said about the information-gathering phase of the sales cycle, but the point I want to leave with you is that 75 percent of the effort and energy we put into the process and 75 percent of the time as well should come before the presentation phase. In addition, a substep follows the information phase that I like to call "verification," in which I confirm that all the material I am going to be putting into the proposal really works for this person. We will be discussing the various ways to do this in the next chapter.

The Verification Substep

Part of the reason we want to spend so much time in the information-gathering phase has to do with closing ratios.

The lower the closing ratio is, the higher the chance that your sales representative is going to succeed over time on the job. The higher the closing ratio is, the more likely he or she is to give up and find another line of work. So, what is the best way to improve closing ratios? The answer is simple: *Never present to a prospect you do not think is going to close.*

If the only thing your staff takes away from your coaching efforts is that they should not invest a lot of time, effort, and energy in developing proposals for people who have not given them clear "buy" signals, your coaching campaign will succeed.

The very best way to insure that you make presentations only to people who are ready and willing to buy from you is to *verify* your information. This is actually quite easy to do, and I am going to include here a few of my favorite strategies for insuring that the information I think I have from the prospect is accurate.

Verify your information in person

This is most appropriate for those situations where your sales process unfolds due to one or two in-person visits. For example, my favorite way of verifying information is to wait until the end of the first meeting as the prospect is walking me to the door. The "business portion" of the meeting is apparently over, and the prospect and I are discussing neutral topics like the weather and the local sports teams. Before I leave, however, I look the prospect in the eye and ask: "Just between you and me, what do you think is going to happen here? Do you think we are going to work together?" The answer I get invariably tells me how much effort and energy I should put into this relationship. In this setting, the prospect sometimes points me toward the other people in the organization I need to talk to before developing a formal proposal. That is invaluable information.

Make a written outline

This is a one-page summary of everything I learned on the first meeting. It contains my key assumptions from the meeting, my timeline for implementation if we were to decide to work together, the product and service recommendations that I am leaning toward, and my pricing range, based on the data. Yes, that is right, it contains just about everything that would eventually go into the proposal, only in much less detail, and in the form of a hypothetical outline of a future document.

That means the prospect is free to tear it up, scribble all over it, tell me I have got everything wrong, or even tell me that it is premature to think about scheduling the dates I have in mind. Notice that the outline takes me about five minutes to put together. It is the reason, typically, that I schedule my second meeting, but it is not a massive time commitment that is out of proportion to the effort the prospect has extended in the relationship. I live and die by outlines, and your sales staff should as well.

Say, "I understand that we are going to be working together"

I've already mentioned the extraordinary power that this sentence has when you deliver it over the telephone after a salesperson has reported a "good meeting" with a given prospect. If your salesperson does not have all the relevant information about the account before you make this call, rest assured that that information will surface after you have this discussion with the prospect.

These are only three of the most common strategies we use for verifying information, but they happen to be the three most effective, and I urge you to instill a philosophy among members of your sales team not to attempt to close the sale and certainly not to attempt to deliver a proposal, unless one or more of these verification strategies has been employed.

The Opening or Qualifying Phase

Let's look at what we have so far.

[ ]	[Information Gathering]	[Proposal]	[Close]
		Verify	(makes sense)
		(substep)	

So far we have a closing phase that is based on the "make sense" preceded by a proposal or reason that makes sense to the prospect.

Where does that proposal or recommendation come from? It evolves from our questions about what this person or operation actually *does* and from the efforts we have made to verify the information *before* creating a proposal.

> The vast majority of your sales team's work must come *before* they attempt to deliver the proposal.

So, these are the three steps of the sales process, including a substep that follows the information-gathering stage. I promised you four steps, though, and that means there is a step that precedes the information-gathering step. As you may have guessed, this step is the opening or qualifying step.

[Opening/Qualifying]	[Information Gathering]	[Proposal]	[Close]
		Verify	(makes
		(substep)	sense)

This is the portion of the relationship when we reach out in the first place, build a little bit of commonality, and determine whether it makes sense for the two of us to talk in the first place. In a face-to-face setting, the qualifying or opening step usually coincides with the first face-to-face meeting. In other selling environments, the first step may take place after we have introduced ourselves on the phone. There is really no hard-and-fast rule about where the qualifying or opening step should unfold, or how, but it *must take place at some point*, because there is no way to gather information from someone we have failed to build rapport and commonality with. There is no way to get intelligent responses to questions when the person we are talking to has not yet concluded that it makes sense to invest time with us.

Sometimes salespeople will ask me how long each one of these steps is likely to take. The answer is, "It takes as long as your ideal selling cycle suggests it should take."

In some telesales environments, I have seen the average cycle for moving through all four of the steps and the information verification sub-step last about five and a half minutes. I have also worked in industrial and governmental selling environments where the process from the left side of the diagram to the right side of the diagram took about a year and a half. The only way to know how long each of these steps "should" take is to monitor closely how long the average sale actually does take in your company.

Three Critical Communication Principles

There are three essential communication principles that your team must master in order to succeed at a high level.

You can help your team master these principles by demonstrating (modeling) all three of them every day in your interactions with your team and then by pointing out how you have done so.

- The sales process (indeed, any process of persuasion) is an extended conversation; we can control the flow of that conversation.

- All responses we hear are in kind; all can be anticipated

- People communicate through stories.

Let's look at these principles one at a time.

1. The sales process is an extended conversation . . . we can control the flow of that conversation.

If I ask a salesperson how she is feeling today, she won't immediately start talking about peach ice cream! **Choose the opening question or statement of any interaction carefully.** The subject you introduce is the point of departure for the rest of the conversation.

2. All responses we hear are in kind, and all can be anticipated.

This is a reliable principle of human interaction that applies to a coaching meeting between a manager and a salesperson, a prospecting call the salesperson makes to a new lead, and the conversation between the prospect and the salesperson that leads to the salesperson's response, "Makes sense to me. What do you think?" **The responses we get in these situations should come as no surprise, and that means we can and should intelligently strategize what happens next.** With just a little experience, we can predict and prepare for the responses we hear every day.

3. People communicate through stories.

People *love* to tell stories—and they often base decisions on what to do next based on their "gut feeling" about the stories we share with them. If those stories match up well with their situation, they are more inclined to listen to us and to trust us. It follows, then, that the more good stories we have to tell people, the more we'll be able to persuade them to take action in a way that we'd like to see. Your goal in any discussion with someone you're trying to build commonality with is **to encourage the other person to tell a story.** One good way is to tell a short story of your own that illustrates a key point, and then to ask for reactions and parallels. Ask whether he or she has undergone similar experiences. **Stop talking and listen.**

Although this chapter is short, I assure you that it contains momentous, career-changing, *life-changing* information for you and your sales team. I urge you to read it, reread it, and then post its contents in a place where you and your sales team can see and reinforce these three communication principles every day.

High Tension, Low Tension

You'll recall, from our definition of "prospect," that any discussion or interaction with someone that does *not* result in a clear Next Step means that person is automatically excluded from the prospect base. There are other places to put such a person (which we'll discuss shortly)—but technically, they can't go into the prospect base, because this person is not a prospect.

This philosophy of sales carries two very important implications:

1. Salespeople *cannot predict income* from people who aren't prospects.

2. Salespeople are therefore highly encouraged, and, with luck, eventually indoctrinated, into a pattern of *making a clear request for a Next Step with a specific date and time.*

Guess what? There is no such thing as instilling this Next Step philosophy without managerial support. As a practical matter, this means that you must get into the habit of *asking* salespeople whether they set a Next Step with their prospective customers and what that Next Step is.

In my experience, if you *don't* ask this kind of question, and the innumerable related questions that accompany it, you cannot expect your team to adopt this mindset in their selling routine.

I have occasionally had salespeople and sales managers object to this system of selling. Perhaps the most common objection is the claim that the type of selling philosophy I'm espousing here is "high-tension" selling—or, to use another phase, "high-stress" selling.

Let's talk for a minute about "stress." If I were to tell you that research in the management-consulting field had established, beyond the shadow of a doubt, that high stress levels had a negative effect on productivity, I don't think you would have any problem believing me. This is exactly what management consultants and researchers over the years have found, beginning with an influential theory developed by the behavioral scientists Yerkes and Dodson that was first published in 1908.

So if high tension results in lower productivity, what do we learn from that finding? Most people will conclude that low tension must therefore result in *higher* productivity. Unfortunately, this is the exact opposite of what Yerkes and Dodson found.

In fact, the low-tension environment is just as *destructive of productivity* as the high-tension environment. A work environment in which there is no stress whatsoever is just as unproductive as a workplace in which there is too much stress or tension.

I think "productive tension" is the tension that is likely to make things happen. Productive tension is the "sweet spot," the middle range of the bell curve.

You have to shake things up a little bit to make anything happen. You can't overwhelm a salesperson, or for that matter a sales prospect, with tension. But if you absolutely abandon the idea of asking for a change in the status quo, nothing will happen!

If we were to compare the levels of tension for a salesperson's meeting with a prospect, a situation of low tension would be asking for *no* Next Step, or for leaving the Next Step vague, as so often happens. (For example, the prospect says, "Let me think about it," and the salesperson walks out the door thinking he has a hot prospect.)

Demanding a Next Step or otherwise badgering the prospect would cause a high-tension situation. (For that matter, it's also equivalent to an inexperienced sales *manager* who is consistently harsh with her sales staff.) Too much stress. That doesn't work either.

The right answer lies somewhere in the middle. We want to promote a culture of *productive* tension in the relationship by asking when, specifically, things are going to happen, and by expecting a commitment of some kind. But we also want to avoid the excesses on either side, either failing to ask for a Next Step at all or by asking for one in a distancing or overaggressive way.

Time and the Selling Cycle

We have seen that the only people who qualify as "prospects" are those who are actively *playing ball* with us. That is to say, they must have scheduled some kind of Next Step with a clear date and time, preferably in the short term, to discuss the *possibility* of doing business. Not every one of these people, however, will agree to do business with us.

In fact, prospects drop out of the base at all times, which means that if I am a sales manager, it is part of *my* job to remind the salespeople that replenishing prospects is part of *their* job. Look at this dynamic a little more closely, and you will see that it matches up with the process classically described as a "funnel" of potential buyers. (In this model, the wide top of the funnel represents the large number of potential buyers, while the small opening at the bottom represents the eventual small number of actual buyers.) For my purposes, I prefer to look at the base as a left-to-right process, rather than as an up-and-down funnel process. This helps me to remember that time, not gravity, is what makes prospects fall out of the system.

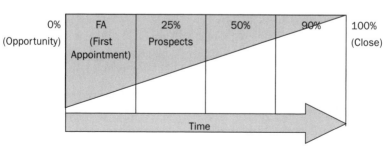

As you can see, time passes, and as it does, our live prospects, the people who are playing ball with us by giving us some kind of Next Step, drop out of the system. In fact, they drop out during a specific period that matches up with my average sales cycle.

This is a difficult concept for many salespeople to grasp, but sales managers tend to understand it intuitively. Their primary challenge then becomes finding an effective way to communicate it to the staff.

Here is what I say:

"The longer a prospect goes out of my average sales cycle, the less likely I am to close the deal."

As I said, salespeople sometimes have a hard time wrapping their heads around this concept, but if you repeat it often and give clear examples, they'll eventually understand what you mean. In the meantime, you can expect them to say things like:

"I closed X deal recently, and it took longer than our average selling cycle."

That may be true, but we are interested in the *average* deal, not in the exception. If we spend our time trying to figure out how to strategize for each exceptional situation, we will have no time left at all. What is important is to figure out what happens *most* of the time, not what *could conceivably* happen.

And most of the time, if we follow a deal that has been in pending status well beyond the period it normally takes for us to close the sale, that deal will evaporate.

Salespeople may also tell you:

"Gee, we sell many different things, and some of them have totally different selling cycles. There is really no use talking about averages."

To the contrary, it is even important to understand the averages for your selling cycle if you handle multiple products and services. Yes, it is quite possible that some of these items will sell significantly faster or on significantly faster or slower cycles than others. That means the salesperson has an obligation to monitor his or her time and effort carefully, and not to continue to invest time, attention, and company resources in prospects who have long since passed their expiration date.

The other day I was talking to a sales manager who supervised a team that had two different products to sell: One product closed in a thirty-day cycle, and the other product typically closed in a twelve- to eighteen-month cycle.

His challenge is getting people who understand that a different approach is necessary in dealing with the thirty-day people than it is in dealing with the twelve- to eighteen-month people!

Sometimes, his team will forget and go back for a fifth or sixth or seventh visit on something that should have been closed by the second face-to-face discussion. On the other hand, it's conceivable that somebody could expect an instant decision when what is necessary is a good deal more consensus building within the account.

> If you do not identify the time cycle for the appropriate situa-
> tion, you cannot measure it; and if you cannot measure it, you
> cannot determine whether it makes sense for you to continue
> trying to sell to that person.

In my company, we have about an eight-week selling cycle. That typically translates to a phone contact to set up the first meeting, a first meeting, a second meeting, perhaps a third meeting to close the deal and any number of phone contacts in between. That's what our average deal looks like.

Am I saying that it *never* makes sense to go on a fourth meeting? No. What I am saying is that I will never go on a fourth meeting *without convincing evidence that the account represents an extraordinary opportunity*—that is, I have to be convinced that I am dealing with a high-dollar account.

All too often, salespeople wend their way slowly through the hallways of the organization, bouncing from supposed decision-maker to supposed decision-maker and wasting weeks, months, even years of company time developing proposals for people who have proved only their unwillingness to buy. Why would we spend our careers looking for such people? Why would we follow their instructions?

If you want to improve your team's performance, *hold them accountable for identifying their own sales cycle.* Then make them *disengage* from the vast majority of situations where they are asked to put in time, effort, and energy beyond that time cycle.

A Million Ways to Say No

We have to remember that there are about a million different ways for prospects to say no. Most of these ways do not actually use the word *no*.

Sometimes, our salespeople are so eager to hear something besides the word *no* that they will hypnotize themselves into believing what they are hearing is yes.

Think of the situation a teenage boy faces in, say, his senior year of high school. He is trying to find a girl who will go out with him, and he picks the prettiest girl in the school. One day, he places his tray next to hers in the cafeteria, strikes up a conversation, and confidently asks if she will accompany him to a movie that Friday night.

The pretty girl smiles and informs him that, unfortunately, she will be washing her hair that evening, but she certainly appreciates him thinking of her.

Cut to the following week. The same guy sits down next to the same girl, strikes up a conversation, and confidently asks her once again if she would like to go out, this time to a baseball game.

She smiles, thanks him, and informs him that on the evening in question, she will be busy rearranging her sock drawer.

Undeterred, the following week the same guy places his cafeteria tray next to the same pretty girl at the same table and confidently asks her if she would like to go roller-skating the following Friday evening.

This time, the girl explains patiently that her aunt Mildred has taken ill, and will require all of her attention for the following six months.

After that first conversation, is it possible that the guy actually believes he is making some kind of progress? After all, the girl has not actually said no. She was very pleasant. She's still talking to him.

But what *should* he have understood after that first discussion?

The answer, of course, is that there are many, many different ways for a pretty girl to say no, and really only one way to say yes: by making a clear commitment to go out at a specific date and time.

In our world, when someone says, "Okay, you can make a presentation in front of the committee," but then does not give us any help in talking to the committee, and makes sure that the members of the committee are *unavailable* to us for the next ninety days, that's a no.

In our world, the act of extending the sales cycle into infinity is also a way of saying no.

This is not to say you do not want to check back with potentially large accounts and try to rekindle the fire. Your team's goal must, however, be to generate relationships that are *currently in progress*, as measured against your average selling cycle. If they're all waiting six months for Aunt Mildred to get better, they're not going to be very happy, and neither are you.

The Triangle

To get the most out of the coaching principles you will be encountering in this book, I urge you to think of the total volume of prospects in your team's base as a triangle. The following graphic breaks the triangle into discrete groups.

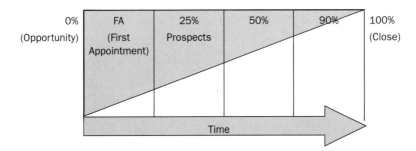

This is the Prospect Management System. This system is the bedrock of the coaching ideas you will learn in this book.

This system is both *date-driven* and *self-correcting*. By date-driven, we mean that every event in the life of a prospect must be dated, and every Next Step that allows it to remain on the board in one of the prospect categories must project forward to a specific future date.

Sometimes I have meetings with sales managers and vice presidents of sales who assure me that they have already implemented Prospect Management System strategies through software patches of one kind or another. They say,

"Steve, we've already got that. We're already doing this, and we're tracking it on our computer."

My response is always: "That's great. Can you please print out a report for one of your people so I can take a look at it?"

Usually the person has no problem doing this and is eager for me to see how perfect his "system" is. So, he dashes off to a computer, prints off a page, and returns with it.

Sure enough, there on the page is a name and company. I point to the company and say, "Okay, this company is one of your prospects, right?"

"Right."

"I'm just curious, when is your salesperson next going to meet with this contact?"

There is usually a long pause. I have yet to find *any* software system that adequately tracks, as a condition of entry to the system, the scheduled Next Step that a salesperson establishes with a decision-maker.

At that point, the person usually mumbles something about wanting to improve the system, and wanting to train his people better.

And that, of course, is where I come in.

It Takes Human Beings

To get someone into the triangle, your salesperson needs to have established a Next Step with the prospect. To keep someone in the triangle, your salesperson needs to keep the prospect relationship moving forward.

I don't care if you use a piece of customized software, a bulletin board, an Excel spreadsheet, a magnetic board, or a piece of slate and a chisel to track the categories in this triangle. What I care about is whether your people are thinking about what's happening next and when.

At the end of the day, this system is not about software, bulletin boards, or magnets. It's about how your sales team thinks. It takes human beings, and specifically sales managers, to *implement* the selling system I am talking about. That's not a technological question, but rather a way of *thinking about the selling process* that can only be brought about, sustained, and reinforced over time by the questions a sales manager asks his or her sales staff.

The next question is: Just what do the category names in the triangle mean?

The Closed (100 Percent) Category

You already know who these people are. The folks on the far right-hand side of the triangle are those who have decided to buy from your company and have completed all the necessary administrative requirements necessary for them to be considered customers. They may be new customers, they may be repeat customers, but they are not *potential* customers. They have accepted the legal language in your contract, or shaken your hand and specified a date of delivery, or arranged with your operations people to begin the switchover from one way of doing things to another.

The specific criteria for inclusion in this category will vary depending on your industry. Just about everybody knows a "closed customer" when he or she sees one.

The 25 Percent Column

This column represents a 25 percent chance of closing the deal.

Think of the people in the 25 percent column as fulfilling the following requirements:

- Your salespeople have met with or spoken with them initially in a meaningful way and have identified how to get the decision made.

- Your salespeople have scheduled an appropriate Next Step with the right people within this organization. Notice that this Next Step is a criterion for inclusion in the prospect base. Please note, too, that your people do not necessarily have to be talking to the highest-ranking people in the organization, but they must be talking to someone who is capable of getting the decision made for them.

- Your salespeople are gathering relevant information and have not yet delivered a formal recommendation or proposal.

If a prospect matches each of these three criteria, he or she deserves to be included in the 25 percent column. Again, how you keep track of the people in these columns is up to you, but at my company we like to do it prominently, using a series of colored magnets to represent the sales team's collective base of prospects on a board that's posted where everyone can see it.

The 50 Percent Column

The next column to the right represents a 50 percent chance of closing the deal.

This is the make-or-break column, and the one that salespeople are most likely to give sales managers arguments on.

To be in this column, your sales team must have fulfilled all of the requirements of the 25 percent column, and have done the following:

- Identified a pricing range that works, although not necessarily the final dollar amount.

- Identified a timing range that works, although perhaps not the final schedule for rollout or delivery.

- Confirmed that the product or service offering is in the right ballpark although some of the specifics may be altered before the final agreement is completed.

Please notice that the 50 percent category still requires that a Next Step be in place, and that the sale does not exceed the average selling cycle for your company when closing deals related to this product or service.

Salespeople sometimes complain that the criteria in this category are too harsh, and that the actual criteria for a 50 percent prospect should sound more like this: "I met with the guy once, and he's thinking about it."

That really does not work for me, and I hope it does not work for you as a sales manager either. Sometimes, I think salespeople would consider buying a lottery ticket to be a fifty/fifty proposition, because there are only two possible outcomes: winning or losing!

By the same token, salespeople sometimes seem to believe that a series of discussions that *could possibly* deliver a sale, or *could possibly* end up collapsing, should, by the same reasoning, be considered a fifty/fifty proposition.

As a matter of cold, hard fact, the criteria outlined here are much better at producing about a 50 percent hit rate for the prospects in question than subjective guesswork from a salesperson about whether there's a fifty/fifty chance of closing the deal. If you or anyone on your team doubts this, just use the system for sixty days, and track your results. If you are like the hundreds of thousands of salespeople we have trained over the years, you will find that roughly half of the people who end up meeting these criteria end up buying from you.

The 90 Percent Column

Look at the next column to the right.

This column is almost as simple as the closed column. It's someone for whom all of the criteria for 50 percent are in place, *and* who has given us a verbal commitment to do business.

Another way of describing this column, and one that is much more likely to get the attention of your salespeople, is what I call the "bet-your-paycheck test."

At this stage, I can look a salesperson in the eye and say, "You're telling me this person's at 90 percent, and that he or she wants to start working with us on April 1. Are you willing to bet your paycheck on that?" If the answer is yes, it's a 90 percent prospect.

Ninety percent prospects, just like 25 percent and 50 percent prospects, require a scheduled Next Step, typically a final meeting or discussion to finalize contract arrangements.

"You Skipped a Column!"

Actually, I didn't skip a column. I just saved the most important one for last.

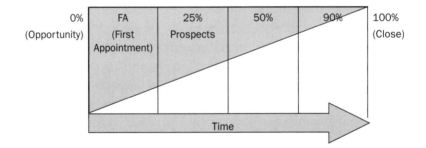

Those 25 percent leads do not just materialize out of thin air. For field sales representatives they arise from a column I call the FA, or First Appointment column.

This column drives all the other activities. In fact, my experience is that every sale that a sales representative closes must be replenished by *five* new entries in the FA column. This is because *it takes many new first appointments to deliver a single sale.*

Let's say, for the sake of argument, that it really does take five new prospects for your sales team to generate a single new sale. Let us assume, too, that the average salesperson on your team maintains twenty "live" prospects this week.

Suppose your salesperson joyfully announces that she has closed a big deal from one of those twenty prospects. It is great news, but it carries a potential downside. That is because your salesperson, if she is like most of the ones we train, will not replenish that prospect. Or, if she does replenish the FA column after closing the sale, she will do so by adding *one* new prospect.

Your salesperson has a ratio of five to one in this area. That means she needs to replace the one prospect who went away with *five* brand-new FAs.

The trouble is that it does not look to your salesperson, or to you for that matter, as though she just used up five prospects. It looks as though she still has nineteen good, solid prospects on the board. But given the mathematical ratios we know to be at work here, those four prospects will eventually desert her; the only question is whether she will notice that they must be replaced before it is too late.

Let's say she does what most salespeople do; that is, she arranges for the final delivery of the goods to her new customer, and uses the various tasks associated with closing the deal as an excuse not to prospect regularly. Suppose, that the following week, with her prospect base looking as though there are nineteen prospects in it, your salesperson closes another deal. The same process plays itself out again. She loses one prospect and thinks she has only lost one prospect, but the ratios suggest otherwise. In fact there are four more prospects from this original base of twenty that she is going to need to replace, but she will assume they still exist.

This process plays itself out continually in the average salesperson's life. The next week, your salesperson might close another deal and believe that she has seventeen prospects, when in fact she only has ten. The following week she might close another deal and believe she has sixteen prospects when in fact she only has five.

Finally, she will wake up some time the following week and all of her prospects will suddenly have evaporated. It will seem like a sudden betrayal, given her extraordinary run of good luck, but in fact, it will only be part of the inevitable, mathematics-driven logic of the sales process. When your salesperson learns that she has been brought down to zero, she will, of course, prospect like crazy in an attempt to rebuild the base. Unfortunately, there are two problems with this. First, it is difficult to do in a short time, which is how most salespeople try to build their prospect base. And second, it is extremely stressful, which means that she is less effective at the other parts of her job, including writing proposals and attempting to close deals. Overall, it is a recipe for diminished effectiveness.

I call this phenomenon the "peaks and valleys syndrome," and the only cure for it that I have ever identified is to make prospecting calls every day, even if—especially if—you have recently closed a sale.

If your sales team has lots of boom and bust cycles, you may want to take a close look at the points I have raised in this chapter and try to hold your people to a "replacement quota"—in other words, require that they close (for instance) one new deal with five new first appointments. If that matches with their actual ratios, and if you enforce the law of replacement over time, you will, as a matter of statistical reality, even out the income cycles of every sales team and expose them to less stressful gotta-get-back-in-the-game sessions of marathon prospecting.

The Opportunity Column

There is one more column to take into account in the Prospect Management System, and that column is known as the opportunity column. It goes to the left of the FA column, which you have just learned about.

The opportunity column is where we put prospects that do not have a Next Step, that we have not yet contacted, or that have for some reason exceeded the average selling cycle for the product or service in question. The opportunity column is not a punishment, nor is it a reflection of poor work on your sales team's part. It is simply a fact. Once somebody falls back to the opportunity column, you and the salesperson are in a much better position to identify what should happen next to that prospect, and you are probably more likely to notice creative ideas you can use to strategize forward movement in the sales cycle.

The Prospect Management System is a self-correcting system, and the opportunity column shows what I mean by that.

If a salesperson and I are having a disagreement about where to categorize a given contact, time is always on my side as the manager. Suppose I say to the salesperson, "ABC Company is a fallback—I'm putting it in the opportunity column."

And suppose the salesperson says to me, "No, no, no—it's really 50 percent. I am halfway there. This is a live deal, it doesn't belong in opportunity." Two things can happen at this point.

The first thing is that I, the manager, can insist that the prospect belongs in the opportunity column, with evidence on my side to support this decision, and the salesperson goes out for the week supremely motivated to prove to me that the prospect is active and moving forward. Isn't that how we want our sales-people to think about their prospects? Don't we want them to be motivated to prove to us that something is happening in the short term?

The other thing that can happen is that I can agree with the salesperson that the prospect does in fact belong at 25 percent, even though putting it there goes against my better judgment. Guess what? If I track the prospects carefully, as both the salesperson and I should certainly do, the matter will be settled for me when we next review his or her sales prospects! Next week, I will be able to say, "Wasn't this the person you told me was absolutely, positively moving forward? What has happened since then? Where is this headed? What's your next step?" At that point, if there are no convincing answers to these questions, it is clear enough that the opportunity column is the proper destination for that prospect.

Sometimes salespeople get all worked up over the opportunity column; that's not a bad thing. If the salesperson hasn't stopped to strategize how he can move this deal forward, placing the lead in opportunity is a great way to focus his attention on what needs to happen next and to generate group discussion.

The Sales Meeting

The system I have just outlined is useless if it is only a matter of abstract classification. If you don't use it, it won't work for your team.

The Prospect Management System only works when it is the focus of a sustained, ongoing series of discussions between you and the sales team. Ideally, those discussions should happen as a group, at a predictable time, once a week. In my experience, these meetings tend to take between a half-hour and ninety minutes, which seems a small enough investment to make for the resulting benefits of the system: namely, a shared vocabulary and a shared interest in working together to identify exactly where prospects stand and how they can best be moved forward.

During these meetings, team members will routinely offer ideas for Next Steps that might help to reawaken a dormant prospect. That's important! I cannot emphasize enough the importance of making these strategy meetings a weekly, or at least regular and predictable, part of your sales culture. If you apply these probing, inquisitive, and frequently skeptical standards to your team's prospect base every three or four months, you won't enjoy the same benefits as the team that makes a habit of *living* by this system. (As a side note, we have implemented this tracking system in virtually every industry, from accounting to waste management, with measurable results in income and retention.)

Managers often ask me to give them some guidance on the best way to run what we have come to call the Monday morning sales meeting, and my answer is always that the meeting should be quite simple. You should work your way around the room, focusing on each person's prospect base, asking, in turn, about prospects who moved from first appointment to 25 percent, from 25 percent to 50 percent, and from 50 percent to 90 percent. In so doing, you should focus on the following questions:

Questions to Ask Salespeople at This Meeting

Here are sixteen critical questions sales managers should learn to ask their salespeople about any pending sale. If managers make a habit of asking these questions during every sales meeting, salespeople will make a habit of finding out the answers before the next meeting.

1. When are you going back (or: talking to this person next)?
2. What does the company do, and who are its customers?
3. Who are you talking to?
4. Why that person?
5. How long has your contact been there?
6. What is this company doing for advertising now?
7. When was the first meeting?
8. Did you call them or did they call you?
9. How much is the deal worth?
10. In your view, what is the very next thing that has to happen for you to eventually close this sale?
11. When and how will you make that happen?
12. Who else are they looking at?
13. Why them?
14. What does your contact think is going to happen next?
15. When is that going to happen?
16. Do they want this deal to happen as much as you do?

You should also make sure your people know the following about every prospect under discussion:

Company name

Name and title of primary contact

Date of first appointment (Very important!)

Dollar value (Estimated value is fine in the early stages)

Next Step

In addition, be sure to track whether this is a new prospect or an existing customer, and how long the prospect has been "pending." The date of your salesperson's first appointment, meeting, or in-depth discussion with the prospect is extremely important. That's when the sales cycle clock begins to run!

(*Note:* I am sometimes asked whether the Prospect Management System will work just as effectively with current customers as with new customer acquisition, or with a hybrid of the two groups. The answer is yes, but it requires some experience on the part of the manager to determine where the priorities should be. Your best course of action is to color-code the various entries into the system, whether they are in a spreadsheet or on a board with physical cards or magnets, with one color representing new business and another color representing established customers. You should also set targets for the balance that you would like to see between new business and old business, if your salespeople are responsible for both, as well as the balance between high dollar-value deals and low dollar-value deals. It is actually quite important to maintain a variety of dollar values in the system; if you have only three or four prospects at 50 percent, and they are all potentially huge deals, you run the risk of instability if for some reason these prospects all drop out over the next week or two—and that is not outside the realm of possibility. Having an additional five or six deals of somewhat lesser value in the prospect base will expose your people to fewer traumatic income shifts.)

The Board Tool

I have already discussed some of the strategies and questions you can use to lead an effective sales meeting. There is one more piece of advice I want to share with you: Study very closely the following board tool. Use it to ask specific questions about particular issues of strategy and prospect placement in the system. Use it to increase the odds that your team will ask their prospects the right questions during sales meetings.

We have had very good success using this tool to "indoctrinate" groups into using the Prospect Management System. At some point, you should yield the floor as manager, and encourage one of your team members to lead the discussion about each team member's active prospect base. You want salespeople to start associating the sales meeting with a certain way of thinking about selling, a question-and-answer-based system of evaluating each active sales lead. This way of thinking can and should be adopted by everyone in the group, not just the person with managerial authority.

Sometimes the managers we work with are concerned that these meetings will turn into free-for-alls when one salesperson or another has the chance to lead the meeting. In my experience, that is quite rare. It is much more common that the team will begin looking at matters more objectively, offering suggestions on how to move important accounts forward and even self-correcting by reclassifying leads downward on their own initiative when they realize they have misclassified something.

Stephan Schiffman's Prospect Management System™ Ranking and Questions Tool

Copyright © 2005 D.E.I. Management Group

	0	FA	1 / 25%
Criteria	■ No next step. ■ No decision expected soon.	■ Scheduled first meeting (date and time).	■ Had FA—now have scheduled next step to gain information.
Questions	■ Why is there no next step? ■ What is happening within the next two weeks?	■ Is this the first meeting about this deal? ■ Is the meeting set?	■ When was the first meeting? ■ When was the last meeting? ■ When is the next appointment?
Strategy Questions	☐ What other companies that are most like our existing customers can we call on? ☐ Whom do our customers buy from and sell to that we can call on? ☐ What percentage of our next opportunities are new customers, former customers, and existing customers?	☐ What are other examples of similar success stories we've had? ☐ Are each day's appointments close together? ☐ Are there any leads near any of these appointments, which would make sense to meet on this trip? ☐ What next step (and fall-back) strategy will you use at the end of these meetings?	☐ What will it take to move this prospect to 50%? ☐ How long will that take? ☐ What would the deal be worth? ☐ What/how/why/when does this company do what it does? ☐ Are they buying from/working with anyone else? ☐ Why that company? How did they choose them? ☐ Is this company looking at any competitor? ☐ Why should they change? ☐ What are the individual decision-makers trying to accomplish? ☐ Can we help them do it better?
Overall Board Management Questions	■ What are the next 11 opportunities to pursue and why? ■ Are there other contacts within our existing prospects and customers worth pursuing?	■ What is the right number of FAs to maintain at all times?	■ What does this column tell us about our recent prospecting activity? A low number would indicate: 1. Not enough FAs in last two weeks. 2. Inability to create a next step with qualified prospects. 3. Small size prospects, which skipped the first stage. 4. Recent FAs were predominantly unqualified (either contact or organization). ■ Is any prospect in this column too old? ■ Do we have a 1-in-4 chance of closing these deals?

2 / 50%	3 / 90%	C / 100%
■ **Presenting to right person with right presentation, right price, right timetable.**	■ **Verbal agreement** ■ **Contract on desk**	■ **Sold, closed**
■ What is the deal worth? ■ Need specific dollar amount. ■ When will they decide?	■ When will this plan close? ■ Need definite date.	
☐ Why are you presenting this proposal? ☐ How do you know this person (or people) will be able to make this decision? ☐ When will they decide? ☐ What is their timetable for implementation? ☐ Who else are we competing against? ☐ Has the specific dollar amount been discussed? ☐ Have the specific plans been discussed? ☐ Do we have a date to present this? ☐ Do they want this to happen as much as you do?	☐ Can you schedule any FAs near these closing appointments? ☐ Does the prospect know they're closing? ☐ Is this meeting merely to close or to advance the sale by beginning implementation? ☐ What specific plan(s) has been selected? Do we have a verbal commitment to do business?	☐ Sold, closed
■ What resources/strategies can be utilized to drive these decisions? ■ If we're waiting for a decision, can we also prospect for new business? ■ Is the value of these prospects multiplied by 50% sufficient to hit short-term income goals? ■ What should the average prospect value be? ■ If too high, the sales cycle lengthens; if too low, prospecting activity must increase. ■ Is any prospect in this column too old? ■ Is there a 1-in-2 chance of closing these deals?	■ Compared to the 50% column, does this column indicate closing skills, presentation, or ranking problems? ■ Is any prospect in this column too old? ■ Do we have a 90% chance of closing these deals?	■ What are the next opportunities within these accounts for more income? ■ When should these opportunities be pursued?

The Levels of the Sales Relationship

Another skill piece I want to share with you before we move on to the issue of implementation has to do with something that is a little bit harder to measure, namely, the level of the sales relationship.

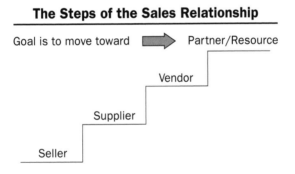

The Steps of the Sales Relationship

Goal is to move toward ➡ Partner/Resource

Vendor

Supplier

Seller

There are four levels in the sales relationship. The higher we move with the customer on the sales continuum, the better our information gets, and the more valuable the relationship becomes over time.

The first and lowest level is the seller level. This level features virtually no trust or information; it's typically a one-time-sale mentality on both sides of the transaction.

The supplier relationship features a little trust and a little information; you're "in the Rolodex," and future business is a possibility but not a sure thing.

The vendor relationship is higher still; it features significant levels of trust and information. There is predictable repeat business, and you help the customer develop criteria for doing business and resolving challenges.

At the partner relationship, there are extremely high levels of trust and information. You function as a strategic partner, and you and the customer are mutually dependent on each other for success. Most of us go back and forth between the second and third levels. If you are in a partner relationship, you have access to all the key players.

The goal of effective selling is to take the time to figure out where we really stand, learn what competitors are involved, and move toward the fourth, or partnership, level.

By the Way ...

If you look closely at the Prospect Management System, you'll see that it corresponds to the three areas of activity we identified in Part I. (You'll learn how to coach for implementation in these three areas in Part IV.)

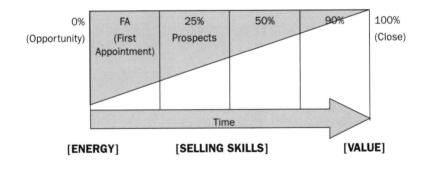

| 0% (Opportunity) | FA (First Appointment) | 25% Prospects | 50% | 90% | 100% (Close) |

Time

[ENERGY] **[SELLING SKILLS]** **[VALUE]**

What We Figured Out in This Section

- The objective of each step is to get to the next step.

- The definition of selling is helping people do what they do better.

- No one "needs" us or what we have to offer; if anyone did "need" us, they would have already called.

- Our number-one competitor is the status quo—what the person or organization is already doing.

- Sell to the obvious by asking how and why the person is already doing what he or she is doing.

- The sales process is an extended conversation; we can control the flow of that conversation.

- All responses we hear are in kind; all can be anticipated.

- People communicate through stories.

- The longer a sale takes out of its normal sales cycle, the less likely it is to happen.

- The key to effective sales is ratios, not numbers.

- Most of the work in the ideal sales process occurs before the proposal, or presentation, of the plan.

- Our close should be a natural outgrowth of the sales process that sounds like this: "Makes sense to me. What do you think?"

- We want the prospect to decide to buy; we don't want to have to sell to the prospect.

- The Prospect Management System will help you track sales activity and will indoctrinate your team to think about the Next Step with each prospect.

- There are four levels to our relationship with the customer.

PART

Are They
Implementing the Skills?

*How can you be sure your people are motivated to implement
what they know about selling . . . not just occasionally but consistently?*

One Principle, Lots of Improvisation

So far, we've been looking at the *strategic* side of the coaching equation—what the goal of the sales process is (to move forward to the Next Step), and *how* salespeople should track prospects in pursuit of that goal. We've been looking at *how* your people can effectively move from the early conversation to the "Makes sense to me. What do you think?" part of the conversation.

This next part of the book is about mastering the *human* part of the coaching equation, which brings us to a difficult question. What is the best way to get salespeople to *implement*, not just occasionally but consistently, what they know about selling?

This "human equation" part of the sales manager's job is, I have to warn you, an imperfect science. It has, to my knowledge, only one principle that is known to deliver positive results without fail. Here it is:

Paying very close attention to a salesperson over an extended period—without judging that person negatively—while looking for (1) things to praise and (2) goals that will inspire him or her to perform *your* view of the job.

That approach does work. You should definitely use it.

Beyond that, though, I can't say with any confidence that anything that follows in this part of the book will *always* work with *every* salesperson. People are funny that way. They only respond positively when they're treated as the individuals they are, and what works superbly for one person can backfire spectacularly when you're talking to another.

So I'm going to insert a "truth in advertising" full-disclosure statement here: Although the next two chapters contain important foundation principles that are relevant to everyone on your sales staff, the goal of those two chapters is simply to get you to ask yourself some critical questions about each of the people on your team. *The answers to those questions are very likely to point you, the manager, in many different directions simultaneously.* Translation: Don't expect a quick fix when it comes to getting people to implement what you want them to implement.

There is, I'm afraid, no magic wand you can wave over your team that will pump them up and keep them pumped up about using specific skills. You, the manager, have to do that job one person at a time. Therefore, your goal should be to find ideas in the pages that follow that will help you work more constructively, *most of the time*, in your discussions with a *single* salesperson. I hope you will use the ideas you find here as a starting point for some inspired one-on-one improvisation with every one of the unique people on your team.

Déjà Vu
All Over Again

At the very beginning of this book, I told you about my typical calling pattern on days when I am not training.

You remember: fifteen dials, seven discussions, and one new first appointment.

You will also recall that my selling process continued, reflecting my ratios in one of three distinct profiles. My daily prospecting activity corresponded to my *energy* profile.

The second level, where I go on five visits a day plus the three follow-up visits, corresponds to my *selling skills* profile.

And the fifty deals a year I close are worth a certain amount of money to me. *How much* money these deals are worth depends on the third element of the sales profile, namely my *value retention skills* profile.

Or, to summarize:

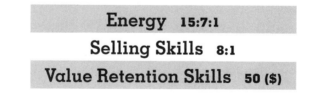

Energy 15:7:1
Selling Skills 8:1
Value Retention Skills 50 ($)

If you haven't picked it up already, let me emphasize that what we're talking about here is *ratios*. How many dials does it take me to create a single first appointment? How many visits do I have to go on to create a single sale?

The key to effective sales is ratios, not numbers.

What you just read is a recap of the key points on selling profiles that we covered at the beginning of the book. Now I want to share with you something new and important that builds on these concepts, something that relates directly to your job as a sales manager. Keep reading!

Applying the Fifteen Coaching Points

Just as an experiment, I'd like you to think, right now, of one of your own sales-people.

Are you thinking of someone in particular on your team? Great. Now, as quickly as you can, I want you to read the following list, and place a check mark in each of the boxes in the checklist **if you think the statement accurately reflects that salesperson's current performance.** (You can do this exercise on a separate piece of paper if you wish. Just number the elements one through fifteen.)

Energy: Setting First Appointments

——— 1. **Understands own ratios.** Is the salesperson monitoring activity ratios on a daily basis? What do the ratios look like? What specific ratio improvement would you like to see?

——— 2. **Has time to complete call targets.** Is prospecting a top priority on the average selling day? Does the salesperson make time to complete prospecting activities on a daily basis?

——— 3. **Number of calls/day steady.** Is the salesperson consistent or are there (for instance) zero prospecting calls for five straight days, followed by thirty or forty calls the next selling day?

____ 4. **Adequate appointments each week.** Is the number of *new* meetings consistent from week to week? Is it the right number, given this person's ratios?

____ 5. **Each first appointment (FA) takes no longer than thirty minutes to set.** How long does it typically take this salesperson to set a first appointment?

Sales Efficiency: The Sales Process

____ 6. **Understands closing ratio.** How many meetings or discussions does it take this person to produce a single sale? Is that the right ratio? Can the salesperson discuss this ratio intelligently with you?

____ 7. **Timeline and sales cycle understood.** What is the average selling cycle on this salesperson's most profitable product/service? Is the salesperson capable of identifying this number without getting distracted by "exceptions" that turned into sales? Does the salesperson understand that what *usually* happens is what determines his or her selling cycle?

____ 8. **Process-oriented (doesn't waste time with dead leads).** Does this salesperson know when to move on?

____ 9. **Masters product knowledge/product malleability.** Can this salesperson make the product or service fit a number of different situations or environments? Has this salesperson ever targeted an entirely new category of prospects?

____ 10. **Takes between sixty and ninety minutes to set and prepare for each follow-up appointment.** Does this salesperson get parallel commitments and input from the prospect *before* committing large amounts of time and energy to proposal development?

Value Efficiency: Price Proposition

____ 11. **Understands pricing structure and margins.** Can the salesperson explain to you the company's margin on what he or she sells? Does the salesperson understand why the different products and services cost what they do?

____ 12. **Able to propose a price that is close to the contract price.** How close is the pricing in the first draft of the proposal to the final pricing?

____ 13. **Takes long-term view of account.** Does this salesperson know when and how to use strategic pricing and bundling skills to close an initial pilot deal with an important prospect—and still make money for the company?

____ 14. **Negotiates from strength, not weakness.** Does the salesperson avoid the trap of discounting without getting something in return? Does the salesperson live by the rule that you should never, ever, offer a discount before a customer asks for one?

____ 15. **Handles price issues honestly and forthrightly.** Does the salesperson stand behind his or her company's pricing, and answer questions directly and with integrity?

As you can see, the three sales profiles break down into five specific sales habits, yielding a total possible score of 15 out of 15.

People who score between 11 and 15 on the checklist are very likely to be above-average performers. Let's call them **Level One.**

People who score between 6 and 10 on the checklist are very likely to be midlevel performers. Let's call them **Level Two.**

People who score between 0 and 5 on the questionnaire are very likely to be "needs improvement" performers. Let's call them **Level Three.**

Look at it again:

Zero to five total check marks: Level Three Performer
Six to ten total check marks: Level Two Performer
Eleven to fifteen total check marks: Level One Performer

Use the Coaching Points for Forecasting

We'll be talking in much more depth about these three groups, and about the fifteen coaching points, in the later portions of this book. For now, though, I want to share with you a shockingly simple strategy, based on the checklist, that just may make your life as a manager a great deal easier.

For years, managers have been complaining to me that the forecasts they receive from their people are always off target. The best way to fix that problem is to project income through the Prospect Management System.

Here's a simplified explanation of how this is done: Add the projected values of everything in the salesperson's 25 percent column in the Prospect Management System. Write down the total. Now multiply that total by 25 percent. Circle the resulting number. Next, add the projected values of everything in the 50 percent column. Write down the total. Now multiply that total by 50 percent. Circle the resulting number. Next, add the projected values of everything in the 90 percent column. Write down the total. Now multiply that total by 90 percent. Circle the resulting number. *Add the three numbers you have circled.* The resulting figure will be your best projection of income over your upcoming selling cycle. In other words, if your selling cycle is eight weeks, and if nothing in any of the columns is misclassified, this process will yield an accurate projection of the income this salesperson will bring in over the next eight weeks.

However, it sometimes happens that managers either haven't indoctrinated their team with the system, or haven't been working with the system long enough to develop meaningful numbers, because the team isn't yet classifying things properly. If you've only learned about the Prospect Management System by reading about it in this book, it's likely that you face one or both of these challenges right now.

Does that mean you are stuck with the numbers your salespeople give you when it's time to pass along a sales projection immediately? As in this week? No. Here's an extremely simple tool you can use to get roughly accurate sales projections *right away* to pass on to senior management, and get on with your day.

- Ask all your salespeople to provide you with a list of *all* of their "live" prospects—that is, the prospects that have agreed to some kind of Next Step in the short term.

- Require each salesperson to assign an *estimated* dollar value to each of these prospects. (If the salespeople complain that they don't yet know how much a given account is worth, ask them to look up the word *estimated* in the dictionary and make their best guess.)

- Put all the prospects from the Level Three people in one pile. Do the same with the prospects from the Level Two and Level One salespeople. Add each of the three piles.

- Take *one-quarter* of the total the Level Three people gave you, and use that number as your projection for a future period that is equal to your next sales cycle. (In other words, if your sales cycle is eight weeks, use that number as your projection for the next eight weeks for the business that will come from the Level Three people.)

- Repeat the process with the Level Two people, but this time take *one-third* of the total the Level Two people gave you, and use that number as your projection for a period equal to your next sales cycle.

- Take *one-half* of the total the Level One people gave you, and use that number as your projection for a period equal to your next sales cycle.

Why should you do this? Three reasons.

Reason #1. It's quick. (Honest. Once you get the numbers from your salespeople, it will take much less time to do what I'm describing than it just took you to read about it.)

Reason #2. It's pretty accurate. (Monitor it over time and see for yourself. It's not as accurate as using the Prospect Management System, but it's certainly more accurate than simply writing down what your well-meaning but occasionally delusional salespeople tell you, adding it all up, and then forwarding *that* figure to your boss.)

Reason #3. It's specific. (No more "range wars"—as in "We should close between forty bucks and half a million bucks over the next eight weeks.")

Try it!

Budget Five Minutes Per Salesperson— and Do This!

53

The Fifteen Coaching Points checklist you just used is extremely important, for reasons that extend far beyond the perennial challenge of generating relatively accurate sales forecasts.

You'll find a copy of this checklist in the appendix. I strongly recommend that you fill out one checklist for each salesperson who reports to you. (If you choose not to do this, you will find that substantial chunks of the rest of this book will be of little practical use.)

During our face-to-face training programs with managers, I *insist* that the participants complete a checklist for every salesperson under the manager's supervision. This should not be a long, drawn-out, data-gathering exercise but should *concisely* reflect your best instant assessment of whether the salesperson in question is already implementing a given sales habit on a consistent basis.

Do this now. Budget a maximum of five minutes for each salesperson. Fill out the checklist for each one. Date the form. Put it in the person's personnel file. Then keep reading.

One More Great Reason Not to Keep Reading This Book Until You've Filled Out a Coaching Points Checklist for Every Salesperson on Your Team

You know how you sometimes dread performance review sessions with certain team members? (Come on, admit it, there *are* people you don't look forward to reviewing.)

If you implement *nothing else from this book*, filling out a checklist for each of your team members will pay off handsomely when it's time to conduct performance evaluations. Consider the following three scenarios.

Scenario One: You sit down with the Salesperson You Would Rather Not Have to Conduct a Performance Evaluation For (hereafter s.y.w.r.n.h.t.c.a.p.e.f.) and, after a little small talk during which you try to be nice and dance around the issues, you either (1) say nothing of substance and hope the person won't notice, or (2) say something like this:

> "Guess what? We're still having some problems we talked about last time. You still have big gaps where you're not closing anything. It happened last quarter and it happened all over again this quarter. You're too streaky. You've got to do better."

s.y.w.r.n.h.t.c.a.p.e.f. either starts fighting with you energetically or walks away mystified about what specifically he or she is supposed to do to make you happy. Once you are out of earshot, he or she says nasty things about you to other people.

Scenario Two: Same meeting, but you say something like this:

> "I read this book, and there was this really interesting exercise I was supposed to do about everybody on my team. I didn't want to do it, but the book made me do it. I literally couldn't keep reading unless I did the exercise for everybody on the team."

(Go ahead, make me the bad guy. I don't care.)

> "Anyway, when I completed this checklist, the first thing I noticed was that you were *extremely strong* in areas *blah, blah,* and *blah.*"

(Exaggerate this a little if you have to. Only show the person the checklist if you think doing so will help the discussion.)

> "By the way, I also noticed that this exercise . . ."

(Not you, of course, but the exercise.)

". . . seemed to suggest we might want to work together on *blah, blah,* and *blah* over the coming ninety days. What do you think?"

You have a productive discussion. You spend five minutes before the next meeting seeing which new boxes you can check off. You date the latest checklist. You file it.

Here's my question. Which of these two scenarios is less likely to leave you feeling lousy after you have your (impossible-to-avoid) meeting with s.y.w.r.n.h.t.c.a.p.e.f.?

Which scenario is less likely to result in you being badmouthed when you turn your back?

I thought so. So let's go for it. If you haven't already done so, stop right now and turn to page 253 of this book. There you will find a blank Coaching Points Checklist. Make enough copies so that you can fill one out for each team member before moving on to the next chapter.

Common Coaching Concerns

An interesting thing happens once you have gone through the process of completing a checklist for every one of the people you manage. You notice certain patterns. If ten people report to you, and six of them show up as Level Two and have always had problems with negotiation skills, you know that is something specific that you need to work on with the team as a whole in terms of *value retention*.

Look at the sheets you've completed for each of your team members.

For the team: **Identify *two* of the fifteen skill areas your team would benefit most from learning, reviewing, or reinforcing.**

You should also take on the same job with specific team members in mind. Look at the team members *individually*.

For individuals: **For each salesperson, identify which *two* of the fifteen skill areas this person would benefit most from learning, reviewing, or reinforcing.**

Do this now for each of the people on your team.

Interestingly, you can learn to predict some common trends for individual performers, depending on whether the person is Level One, Level Two, or Level Three. (*Note:* What follows is not going to be universally true for all salespeople within each of these levels, but the general trends for each level are certainly worth knowing about.)

Common Skill Challenges for Level Three Performers

I've talked to literally thousands of sales managers who spent most of their time figuring out how to address the performance problems associated with Level Three performers. In fact, this group takes up most of a sales manager's time.

There are a few extremely important things to say about Level Three performers:

- They fall into two categories: People who are probably going to *stay* in Level Three and people who are clearly on their way *up* to Levels Two and One. (Come on, you know it's true. Not only that, you probably know instinctively *which* of your Level Three people will grow as a salesperson and which won't.)

- Sometimes, sales managers *can* afford to replace the lowest-performing Level Three people with new people who are likelier to grow in the job, but sometimes they *can't* do that.

- Regardless of whether they eventually improve enough to move up to Level Two, a significant number of Level Three people *can* improve their skills enough to be what might charitably be referred to as a "high-functioning" Level Three performer. (There is a difference between someone who exhibits one out of five *energy* traits and someone who scores five out of five.)

Managerial concerns about Level Three performers tend to focus on one specific skill issue. Can you guess what it is?

Many—and perhaps most—Level Three performers do not prospect enough.

I have included in the appendix an article titled "The Nine Principles of Cold Calling" that is likely to be of interest to managers of Level Three performers who have prospecting challenges. In addition, you may want to encourage your salespeople to read my book *Cold Calling Techniques (That Really Work!)*, which is too detailed to summarize here.

Common Skill Challenges for Level Two Performers

Just as there are predictable challenges with Level Three performers, the managers I work with tend to say predictable things about the Level Two people who report to them.

Here's a very common challenge managers tend to report about this group:

Many Level Two performers do not know how to run a meeting.

Actually, this is also true of most Level Three performers, but managers tend to realize that the prospecting problem is potentially much more serious in the short term, so that's what they tend to focus on first, and rightly so.

For those performers who have problems running a meeting, you can read, distribute, and discuss the following articles, which also appear in the appendix:

- The Next Step: An Overview (page 237)
- Sixteen Ways to Ask for a Next Step (page 240)

I make it a rule that salespeople never leave the scene of a meeting or conversation with a prospect without at least asking for a Next Step. You should, too.

Common Skill Challenges with Level One Performers

Although there are predictable patterns and common challenge areas for performers in the Level Three and Level Two categories, my experience is that Level One performers tend to present coaching challenges that are very hard to predict. This group can be tricky. Your goal is to make sure they still feel challenged to grow professionally, but you also have to grant them a certain amount of autonomy. They've earned it.

As a broad but *general* rule, those people in this group who do need skills coaching are likely to benefit most from coaching in the area of negotiation.

Of course, Level Three and Level Two people are likelier to be *worse* at negotiation than Level One people. It's rare for people in the bottom two groups to score well in the Value Retention Profile. Not impossible, but rare.

With that in mind, consider the discussion that follows, which is designed for managers who must coach Level One performers, or anyone else, out of the common habit of discounting instinctively.

I believe that this discounting problem arises from a survival instinct. Salespeople somehow learn to associate, deep in their central nervous system, pleasure with discounting quickly—or even volunteering to discount the price.

They come to see this as an effective way to close the sale and win the loyalty of customers.

The problem is that they are usually not comparing this strategy to anything else. Like, say, asking an intelligent question and staying silent until the prospect answers. I have a feeling that simply asking the prospect, "Why do you say the price is too high?" or "What price did you have in mind?" and then closing your mouth would stave off the vast majority of unnecessary discounts.

One evening I received a telephone solicitation from a salesperson whose goal was to sell me a home improvement product. I cannot even remember which one it was. Let's say, for the sake of argument, that it was a carpet cleaning service. I listened politely to the salesperson's appeal, and decided that I did, in fact, want to buy what he was selling. So, I said a single word: "Sure."

Do you know what he did? *He offered to discount the product for me!*

That's right. He had been so conditioned by calls where he encountered price resistance that he actually interpreted my "Sure" as a request for a lower price, even though I was asking him to sign me up!

I think a lot of needless discounting happens in much the same way. The salesperson realizes that he or she is getting close to the finish line, and assumes that knocking 33 percent off the top is a valid strategy (and maybe the only strategy) for finalizing the deal.

Let me share some last thoughts with you on the challenging task of coaching the Level One performer.

- Your interactions with this person *should not* be based on checking his or her work closely, every day, to make sure the salesperson has crossed every *t* and dotted every *i*. In fact, the Level One performer is likely to resent this treatment. This is where many of these relationships go wrong. Sometimes managers do not realize that a superior performer must be treated a little differently than a brand-new recruit.

- Never forget: If the person scores at 14 or 15, and is one of your top performers, your job is to *keep him or her from jumping ship*. It is far, far easier to hold on to a great salesperson than it is to recruit or train one into existence.

- Find out whether this contributor is willing to work with less experienced salespeople, and to serve as a role model or mentor. Some of the people at Level One will respond quite positively to this opportunity; for others, interacting with people who have significantly less experience or income potential will be seen as a punishment. If the person would be more likely to accept the mentor role as validating his or her expertise, consider pairing this top performer up with a colleague who isn't quite performing at Level One.

Anybody You Coach May Forget about Prospecting

Prospects drop out of the Prospect Management System as time passes, which is why replenishing the First Appointment is so important!

There is some number, greater than one, by which your team members must replace "live" prospects whenever they close a sale. The closing ratio may be eight to one, or three to one, or five to one. I don't know what it is, but I can guarantee you it isn't *one* to one, and that means your people have to be reminded constantly to replenish their prospect base according to their own closing ratio.

When a Salesperson Prospects Religiously, Then Stops When Things Get Busy

Let's say you are coaching a salesperson whose categories in the Prospect Management System currently fall into the present formation:

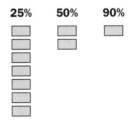

Actually, this is (broadly speaking) the ideal formation. Forget about the number of prospects for a minute: The ratios of one group to another are right. Out of each ten prospects, seven are in the 25 percent column, two are in the 50 percent column, and one is nearly closed in the 90 percent column. The person is setting first appointments and prospecting proactively for new business. So, if your salesperson keeps up this formation on a regular basis, there will be a constant stream of income.

But, let's say, this person's normal sales cycle is four weeks, and this person stops prospecting. What will things look like a month from now?

After a month of no prospecting, here's what the person's prospect base looks like.

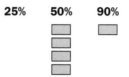

Let's face it. If you, the manager, lose focus and let this happen by failing to ask about daily prospecting, your salesperson's going to have to work like crazy to catch up. That's going to be extremely stressful for both of you!

When a Salesperson Is Distracted by Deals That Are about to Close

Suppose your salesperson had this formation:

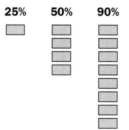

What's going to happen in the short term? Of course, many deals are going to close, which seems like good news, right?

Maybe. Now ask yourself what this person's world is going to look like four or five weeks from now. There's going to be a crisis! There will be nothing to close, and nothing getting ready to close. (This is a very common formation, by the way; the only antidote is regular application of quality prospecting time.)

When a Salesperson Has a 90 Percent Drought (The Question Is *Why?*)

What about this situation?

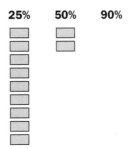

My question for the manager of this salesperson would have to do with why this person has nothing new closing, with all these prospects at 25 percent. It's possible that the person just closed a whole bunch of deals and then realized it was time to set some appointments. If that's *not* what's going on, then the manager should probably sit down with this person and figure out what, specifically, went wrong on the last few deals. If there's a problem with selling skills, the manager should have a sense of what those are and build a personal coaching plan around them.

When a Salesperson Needs a Reality Check

How about this situation?

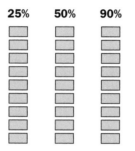

In the real world, no salesperson would even have time to complete all these sales. Something's wrong with the formation here, because as you move through the process, prospects should fall out and the board should have some variation. This looks like a prospect base that hasn't been updated recently. Either that, or the salesperson isn't classifying things properly. Whichever it is, you need to institute a reality check of some kind during a one-on-one coaching session.

The Four Ways to Coach Salespeople

Just about any "manager" can sit back and take notes on what the members of her team are doing. It takes a different approach, I believe, to get involved in the person's world and take the steps necessary to **change what actually happens in that world**.

Let me be more specific. In my experience, it takes work in four specific areas to become that second type of manager. In the following chapters, you will learn about each of these four critical activity areas for sales managers.

- Motivation
- Communication
- Training
- One-on-one coaching sessions

Let's look at each area.

Motivation

This underlies everything. In a coaching context, motivation means harnessing existing motivators within your salespeople. The most obvious motivators are:

Fear (ineffective over the long term)

Incentive (not just monetary)

Growth (the most important of the three)

Fear does not work over the long term. Relying solely on monetary incentives doesn't work over the long term. Appealing to personal growth goals is the most important motivator.

My company once worked with a salesperson who was struggling in his first months on the job. This salesperson's father was convinced that his son had made a major career mistake in taking a job in selling. We helped set up a powerful goal based on meaningful incentives, personal growth, and on what was *already* important to him.

So the manager said, "If you hit x dollar target this month, I'll take your dad out to breakfast and explain what a great job you've done this month."

It worked!

It's all a question of positioning. If you must focus on money, focus on what the money will *mean* to the salesperson. If someone is getting married soon, don't just talk about a bonus, consider setting up a sales goal of "$4,000 for your honeymoon." If someone is saving for a house, gear the commission goal to the down payment.

Communication

This means mastering (and modeling) the three critical communication principles we discussed in Chapter 37. If you do that, you will, by definition, be listening effectively and conveying the right information in the right way.

If you don't communicate effectively, the salesperson won't understand what's expected of him or her.

Communication takes place on two levels: verbal and nonverbal.

According to a study in the *Journal of Consulting Psychology*, this is how face-to-face communication is interpreted:

- 7 percent verbal

- 38 percent tone of voice

- 55 percent body language

What does your body language say about your relationship to the salesperson? What does his or her body language say about the way your message is being received?

Training

Formal training can take the form of an instruction session for the group as a whole. Informal training can take the form of working with an individual salesperson to solve a specific problem. (See the section on one-on-one coaching.)

In both situations, we're defining a certain issue and training the salesperson in the skill sets necessary to resolve challenges.

If you don't identify problem areas and train effectively, you will never know whether the salesperson has the right skills to hit performance targets or grow in the job.

One-on-One Coaching Sessions

Mentoring during one-on-one coaching means monitoring performance over time and "selling" the relevant techniques, skills, goals, and concepts necessary for ongoing growth.

If you don't coach, mentor, and monitor on a regular basis, you won't know how—or whether—the salesperson is actually implementing the skills she has developed.

Here are some key questions I ask managers about their one-on-one coaching programs:

- How often do you have coaching sessions?

- Who initiates the sessions?

- When was the last session?

- What issues did you discuss?

- What next step did you set?

- How do you know the person took action?

Monitoring and coaching performance over time is an essential component of an effective coaching plan. The more predictably coaching and follow-up sessions occur, the more likely positive change is to take place. If you only call a meeting when there's a serious problem, your team will learn to associate coaching meetings with negative performance and confrontation—with negative effects on team performance! If, on the other hand, you make regular meetings a part of your routine, everyone will have a good idea of what is taking place in the department and where improvements must occur.

When you do this part of the job right, you *know with certainty* whether the salesperson is implementing learned skills.

To run an effective coaching meeting, you must know exactly in which area you want the other person to improve; otherwise, the meeting will focus only on intangibles.

Over-reliance on intangibles (like "Do the best you can to build up your contact base") may build resentment or antagonism on the part of the salesperson.

Consistent success in sales depends on *benchmarked* progress in specific areas. If you're looking for specific benchmarks to measure, the fifteen coaching points are the best place to start.

Common Salesperson Personality Types

I have found that managers tend to face similar challenges from particular, recognizable subgroups of salespeople. In other words, whether the industry in question is semiconductors or insurance, obstacles to the face-to-face coaching process tend to take predictable forms within certain groups.

For lack of a better label, I call the most common of these forms "personality types." It is not, strictly speaking, an accurate label; there are certainly detailed, tested personality models that will tell you more about the person's way of looking at the world at large. But in terms of identifying the way the person looks at the job of selling, which is what we are most concerned about here, I think the following chapters will be helpful.

In the following chapters, you will find a summary of each of the main sales personality styles I have identified, as well as some advice on how to have constructive interactions with someone who fits that description.

Personality Type: *The Boxer*

What you may hear: "It's not my fault."

How to handle this person: Focus on ratios and numbers, not anecdotes. If you allow yourself to be drawn into the details of the story the person is fixating on, you'll get sidetracked.

When dealing with a salesperson who immediately goes into defensive mode by offering excuses, stories, or nonwork-related tales of woe, disengage and be ready to ask, "So, how are you doing on your daily target for completed calls? What are you going to do about that today?"

Or: "Mark, you and I have been working together since February 1 after I called the team together and told everyone that we were going to be tracking these numbers, and here are your numbers. I think you have done a great job in collecting them" (or "I think you are getting a lot better in terms of collecting them than you were a month ago").

"And here is what I want to talk about. . . ."

At this point, I go around to his side of the desk to eliminate some of the teacher/student or parent/child dynamic that may be keeping real communication from happening and to help us to communicate as colleagues. Figuratively, this move to the other side of the desk means that I have my arm around Mark's shoulder. I may not actually put my arm around his shoulder, given the restrictions Human Resources Departments follow these days, but the act of moving over to Mark's side is a very positive and bonding element that roughly equates to putting my arm around his shoulder. The point is that Mark and I are going to work together and look at his numbers to see if we can improve one thing. And if our new idea works, we will both pick that up. If it does not work, we will pick that up and we will try something else.

If I move over and sit side by side with a defensive person, it is a lot less likely that the discussion is going to become paralyzed. And, by the same token, if the topic is the numbers for his own dollars and completed calls and appointments, then there is really nothing that we can argue about, especially if Mark himself collected the numbers.

59 Personality Type: *The Riddler*

What you may hear: ambiguous remarks ("That all depends") or unexpected and unexpectable questions ("What I really want to know is . . .").

How to handle this person: Stay focused on the question or issue you've posed. *Politely* repeat it as necessary.

When dealing with a salesperson who tries to hijack the conversation or avoid questions, you have to return patiently to the issue you've raised. For instance: "That's an interesting issue, and it's something we may want to address later, but right now what I think we want to look at is. . . ."

Not too long ago, we had a salesperson named Cathy on our team. I'd say to Cathy, "Where is the two o'clock meeting going to take place?"

Cathy would answer, "Well, it's going to rain today."

Then there would be silence and I would stare at her and wonder what was going on in the conversation.

I'd ask again and try to cover for the non sequitur that she just gave me. Then I'd say, "Just so we can be clear, is the building on the East Side or the West Side? That's all I am trying to figure out."

And she'd say, "They think it is going to rain actually for the early part of the day, and then it will turn to sleet in the afternoon."

All right, I'm exaggerating, but only a little. The fact of the matter is that you can't get a straight answer out of some salespeople. The best person who ever did that deliberately was probably President Clinton. He was a genius with the way he would not answer the question. And he used a rhetorical device that is worth understanding if you are ever trying to deal with a Riddler salesperson. If you asked President Clinton a question and he did not want to answer, he would say, "Let me recap that question, so we can get to the core point that you're really asking about." And then he would pose a different question, one that he was presumably prepared to answer. And then he would answer that question.

While President Clinton was doing that sort of thing deliberately, and doing it quite well, I think a lot of these Riddler salespeople operate on two levels. Sometimes, I think they use the speaks-in-riddles approach as a defensive mechanism, but sometimes I do not think they realize what they are doing. In fact, they may not even realize the important issue that the manager has brought up or its true importance. The net result is that if you follow the Riddler's lead, you will eventually find that you are talking about something entirely different than what you want to focus on. It is frustrating and can sometimes lead to tension between the manager and the salesperson.

So one of the things you have to do with salespeople in general, and Riddlers in particular, is *tactfully* return the conversation to the very topic that was raised the first time around. This is more difficult than it sounds, because if you are less than tactful, it is going to sound as though you are either challenging the person, or insulting his or her intelligence, or both.

Every time Cathy came back from a meeting, I was prepared to pose a certain sequence of questions, a sequence I asked *every time we were in that situation*, so Cathy knew to prepare for it ahead of time and knew that she was going to be asked, directly but politely, about each of those issues.

The trick is to refuse *politely* to let the Riddler off the hook until the discussion moves forward in the direction that you have established, and to do so in the same way repeatedly.

After just a few conversations, the Riddler will learn that the questions are not going away and she really does have to prepare for them.

For instance:

- Who did you meet with?
- How long has the person been with the company?
- What does the company do?
- What does the person do?
- What was this person doing before they had this job?
- Who are the company's competitors?

And so on.

We have a saying at my office: "They will respect what you inspect." In other words, if I make it part of my routine to ask what the decision-maker's previous job was, then eventually the salesperson will pick up that this is a specific piece of information that I need and will get it for me just about every time.

Personality Type: *The Yes-Person*

What you may hear: "Absolutely!" (This team member will yes you to death.)

How to handle this person: Role-play the specific actions you want this person to perform. Don't assume that yes means this person can or will do as you say. Ask for evidence: "So what are the first three questions you're going to ask at the meeting?"

This is the "Yes You to Death" salesperson. Suppose you say "Listen, we're going to have to move the whole building three feet to the left. Can you do that for us?" These people say, "Yeah, sure, no problem."

The "Yes You to Death" approach is often a cover for the following message: "I'm really not listening at all."

In fact, the meaning could be a cover for this message:

"I know what I'm doing already, and I really would rather not have any communication with you, my manager, so I'm going to nod my head like this until you go away."

Let me give you an example. Sometimes, we have extended training sessions that are focused on improving closing skills. For one of the strategies we share, we tell salespeople:

> "When you go to the second meeting, and you know the person hasn't seen your pricing before, and you think that it may be an issue, here's what I want you to do. I want you to walk in the door, walk up to the person and, after you've shaken hands and said hello, say, 'Mr. Prospect, when we finished our last meeting, let me tell you what I did. I went back to my office and I talked to my boss. I talked to our communications director, and I talked to

our VP of Operations. I talked to the whole team. I put together a detailed plan based on the goals we discussed last time, which are *A, B,* and *C.* I love it, and I think you are going to love it. But I think you are going to have a problem with the price.'

"And then I want you to turn the paper over and slide it across the desk face-down so the prospect has to pick it up and look at the price and then give you a response. *Don't say anything* after you slide the paper. The prospect is going to pick it up, look at the price, and give you a more-or-less honest reaction to what the pricing looks like, whether it is okay or problematic for some reason. You will get a good discussion going about pricing that way. So that's what I want you to do."

That technique does work, by the way. Now why do I bring this up in reference to the Yes-Person? Because during one particular coaching session, the person I was training to do this kept telling me, "Yes, yes, I've got it," when in fact I needed to understand what the person was saying as, "Please role-play this with me until I could do it from a coma." It only *sounded* like, "Yes, yes, I've got it."

The idea was to get that discussion going with the prospect, and then, when you get pushback, continue by asking, "Okay, how far off am I?" You can actually get most of your negotiating done up-front as opposed to waiting until the last moment. What's more, you will get a significant indication of the person's interest by watching what happens when she sees the price. If looking at the price makes her keel over and grab her heart, then you know that you have probably gone in too high. If, however, the person calmly nods and says, "Hmm . . . I see what you mean," that's an entirely different discussion. Now, did the salesperson I was coaching understand all this? Perhaps intellectually, but he wasn't ready to implement it.

I went through that whole performance, including the final element of saying, "Okay, we're $2,000 apart, what if I do this other way, would we have a deal?" I acted it all out for the salesperson. Then, when I showed up for our coaching session the following week, I asked how the meeting had gone. The salesperson tried to change the subject.

Bad sign.

It turned out he hadn't done any of the stuff we had discussed, despite his constant assurances that he "got it." Absolutely none of it had stuck. So, he hadn't used any of it. In fact, he got sidetracked after the small talk, let the prospect drive the whole meeting, and walked out without having gotten any meaningful discussion going about the price. What he got was: "Hmm, this looks interesting. Let me think about it."

That was what we were trying to avoid by scripting out the whole opening.

With the Yes-Person, you have to role-play repeatedly until it becomes hard-wired what he or she is supposed to do in a given situation. (By the way, that's exactly what I did, and the salesperson closed the deal on the next meeting.)

Personality Type: *The Know-It-All*

What you may hear: "You just don't understand!" (Or some variation.)

How to handle this person: Focus on ratios—not on the person—and ask for input.

This team member is usually—but not always—older than you are. Before you start a fight, try coaching *first* by asking for insight and advice.

I had this kind of a meeting with a newspaper advertising salesperson who had been with the paper for a long time. He had, quite literally, no prospects. His boss said to me, "Can you demonstrate to him how important the Prospect Management System is?"

There are many ways I could have opened that meeting. "Your boss thinks this system is important for you to implement, and you've got to get more first appointments." Or "You realize you have no prospects, right?" Or "What the hell are you doing?"

I could have opened the meeting by saying one of those things. But would any of those have been the *best* to say? Of course not.

What was the best thing to say?

Here is what I did say.

- "How long have you been in sales?" (Answer: Ten years.)

- "Okay. My guess is that you are pretty good at what you do. That is probably the assessment you would have, right?" (He agreed, and actually looked flattered.)

- "Okay—let's pretend that you're the manager and I am the salesperson. I just handed you this activity report. What would *you* say to me?" (Now he was forced to put on his know-it-all cap and answer me.)

Guess what? He gave me a great answer. He did a complete analysis of what someone would have with a board that looked like his. He gave a superb coaching critique of somebody who knew the prospect better and who had the prospect on a consistent basis.

I said, "That's it. What you just said is your best advice. I could not possibly top it. You do not need me to tell you what to do, just execute what you just told me, and let's make a note to check back in a month to see how it's going."

He started using the system!

Personality Type: *The Blamer*

What you may hear: "I don't get support from. . . ." (Or:) "So-and-so made a mistake, not me."

How to handle this person: Get this person direct experience with the other people or departments in the organization. Get the Blamer involved in the relevant meetings and discussions.

When dealing with a Blamer, ask for "help" that will broaden his or her experience base: "I'd like you to sit in on a meeting with the people in accounting on how to deal with some collection issues. Can you help them brainstorm this afternoon?"

One of the best ways to deal with a Blamer is to confront her with the person she's most likely to blame. I've coached Blamers who lived to create feuds on the job. A strange thing happens when you assign *both* participants of a feud to work together on an important account. Either one of them quits (which may not be that big of a problem, when you think about it), or they learn to work together.

Personality Type: Cancer

What you may hear: Rumors, innuendo, and so on.

How to handle this person: If you can, isolate this person from other members of the team. If ongoing disruptive behavior persists, consider taking steps toward firing him or her.

When dealing with this kind of salesperson, set limits and do your best to minimize his or her influence on the group. ("Rather than send Tom with you, I think you and I should strategize on how to handle the meeting with ABC Company.")

Let's face it. Some people are so relentlessly negative that they make other people negative and affect them with their negativity. The best first step with these people is to separate them—that is, physically move them out of the office. (These days, so many people are telecommuting that this isn't that big a deal.)

If for some reason that doesn't work out, you should consider working with your Human Resources department to find a way to begin termination proceedings.

> If you are absolutely, positively certain you cannot turn Cancerous salespeople around, and they're not superior contributors, get rid of them.

Personality Type: *Me Now*

What you may hear: "Why bother?" (Or:) "This is boring."

How to handle this person: Understand that this person may have trouble linking short-term performance with long-term rewards. His or her attention span may be short. Work with this person to develop personalized goals; emphasize, on a daily basis, the rewards for engaging in the right activities.

When dealing with a Me Now salesperson, emphasize every day the rewards for engaging in the right activities. For instance: "How many more appointments do you need today to stay on track for that sports car you want?"

When a Me Now person undertakes a career as a salesperson, there's an immediate challenge. After all, the work we do today does not really do anything for us today. If they do not get gratification for what they are doing today, they are not very interested. Why should they work hard today when it's not going to pay off for weeks or months?

The best advice I can give you in dealing with Me Now salespeople is to get close enough to them as a colleague to help them set goals that really inspire them, and then constantly appeal to those goals during one-on-one meetings, and reinforce, with plenty of evidence how today's activity connects with the goal. That advice applies to all salespeople, of course, but it's particularly important to make the evidence vivid and dramatic when you're dealing with this group.

It's easier said than done, of course. Some more detailed advice on setting goals appears near the end of the following chapter.

The Art of Running the One-on-One Coaching Meeting

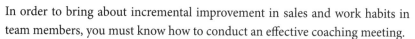

In order to bring about incremental improvement in sales and work habits in team members, you must know how to conduct an effective coaching meeting.

Here's the big secret about these meetings. *The less often you have them, the worse they go.*

Conversely, *the more often you have them, the better they go.* So if you plan to orchestrate and reinforce an ongoing coaching program, schedule these one-on-one meetings at short intervals (say, once a month), post the schedule where everyone can see it, and *then stick to it.*

If you only call coaching meetings when there's a crisis, then the person will learn to associate negative emotions—stress and conflict—with the coaching process. On the other hand, if you schedule coaching meetings regularly, it will be comparatively easy for you and the salesperson to work together to address the most important ongoing issues.

Here are the five steps of the successful coaching session.

Step 1: Know the Team Member

Before evaluating performance, take time to understand the salesperson. Why is the person in this job? Does he or she want to grow? Is this person here for the short or long term?

Step 2: Observe/Evaluate the Person's Work Habits and Sales Skills

Do a Value Scales checklist on this person (see Chapter 51 and the appendix). Before your first coaching meeting, ask the salesperson to write down five strengths and five weaknesses he or she brings to the job. Compare this list to your list, and discuss the differences.

Step 3: Plan the Approach

Develop an agenda for the coaching session. Limit yourself to *one* objective (e.g., to help the representative develop better rapport with account contacts during the first face-to-face meeting. Anticipate the representative's objections and prepare your own turnarounds/responses. Most important, decide on a strategy for the coaching session—just as you would for a sales call. How will you open the meeting? Where will it take place? How will you adjust for this person's personality or working style? I cannot emphasize how important it is that you know exactly how you will open the coaching meeting. Remember, when we control the flow, all responses can be anticipated. (*Note:* Because planning the approach to the coaching meeting is one of the most important things you as a manager can do, I'm going to give you some more specific advice in the next chapter.)

Step 4: Coach

Discuss why you are having this meeting, what you would like to accomplish, and what you have observed. Listen to the salesperson's side *first*. Let the salesperson explain and discuss what has happened from his or her perspective.

> During the one-on-one coaching meeting, listen to the salesperson first.
> If you do not do this, *the salesperson will not listen to you.*
> (Remember, people respond in kind.)

Then and only then, you can explain your perspective on the situation; then you can explain what changes can help.

When your turn to talk comes around, the trick is to avoid stating issues—whether they are positive or negative—as stark facts, but instead clearly label your assessment of what is going on as a biased and imperfect understanding. It is particularly important to do this with salespeople who have put up roadblocks to working with you. There is no real advantage in trotting out "facts" that you know will be instantly challenged, so why bother? Instead of getting into a conflict about who gets to determine the reality of the situation, label your understanding of the situation as your perspective and your perspective alone. If you can do so while finding something—anything—to praise in the salesperson's performance record as a means of opening the conversation, you will have gone a long way toward establishing a productive dialogue during the coaching meeting.

Here's what it might sound like: "Well, from what I can see, your prospecting skills are superb; your interviewing questions just need to be fine-tuned a little bit. . . ."

The beauty of this approach is that you leave yourself the option of closing your assessment with a request that the salesperson then offer his or her assessment for the same issue you just raised. It's the salesperson's turn to talk. "That is what it looks like from here, but how do you see it?"

Be sure you get agreement. Get agreement/verification on what the problem is, and what can be done to solve it.

If you have done your work correctly, have avoided pointless confrontations, and have found legitimate reasons to praise the salesperson's work up to this point, you should have relatively little trouble getting agreement on what, specifically, needs to happen next.

This is perhaps the most critical phase of the coaching meeting, and the one that managers are most likely to overlook. Perhaps we believe that, having established some kind of rapport with the salesperson concerning the performance areas that need work, it is only a matter of common sense from this point forward. Surely, the salesperson would not invest the time and energy in a discussion like this without following through to address the problems that have been uncovered!

If only it were that simple. In fact, the specific Next Step we set here with the salesperson is just as important as the Next Step we ask him or her to set with prospects. In fact, it is probably more important, because productive long-term changes in sales teams only come about when the members of the staff know that they are going to be held accountable for specific, measurable actions. This brings us to . . .

Step 5. Follow-up

Make sure that the meeting does not end until you and the salesperson have reached some clear agreement on the specific action to be undertaken before the next meeting. It might be making four more dials per day. It might be consulting with you on any proposal with a dollar value over $20,000. It might be giving you the names of key contacts within a specific major account, so you can call to introduce yourself and congratulate the new prospect on a good meeting with your salesperson.

Whatever it is, make sure that the next step you identify is:

- Comparatively easy for the salesperson to fulfill. (Not too hard, but a bit of a stretch and a change of the current habit you are trying to alter and a change in the status quo he or she is used to employing in this area.)

- Measurable. (How will you know when this has taken place?)

- Connected to a specific timeframe. (When will you next discuss this issue with the salesperson?)

- Connected to a clear payoff for the salesperson. (Does this person want to win an award? Get married next year? Show a family member that he's a success? Save up for a Corvette? **Identify a personal goal that fires this individual, and then connect a measurable *daily* activity to that payoff.**)

The performance goal you negotiate with the salesperson should be doable but a stretch.

Develop a specific written plan with a timetable for completion and follow-up.

> The plan you set up has to be for an appropriate interval for the topic and the person. If the salesperson helps you to create the plan, you will have little or no pushback. If the plan is perceived as something you are attempting to impose on the salesperson, it is unlikely to work.

The plan of action you eventually come up with should not sound like this:

"You're only making six dials a day, and that needs to be ten dials a day, so let's check in on this in a year."

Nor should it sound like this:

"You're not closing big enough deals. Let's revisit this issue in ten minutes."

You can only find the right balance by holding regular meetings with the team member.

Both the coach and the salesperson should set aside a certain specified period to focus only on coaching issues related to this plan. (I recommend a minimum of fifteen minutes a week.)

> Be sure you follow through on coaching meetings that you
> schedule. Have them when you say you will have them. This is
> very important. Otherwise, this is the only lesson salespeople
> take away from the process: "If you hold your breath for a
> week, it all goes away."

More on the One-on-One Coaching Meeting

In order to run a successful one-on-one coaching meeting, you should be sure to do the following:

- Know your opening.
- Get to the point.
- Talk about ratios.
- Stay away from words that make people freeze up.

Let's take a closer look at each of these tips.

#1: Know Your Opening!

Have you ever absolutely lost track of the goal you had in mind during an important discussion?

If you're like me, you can think of a time when you had an argument or discussion with someone, a discussion that you knew you had to win, but you were not sure exactly what point you were trying to get across. Often this happens during a fight with a spouse or a significant other. It might begin because of a disagreement about whether the toothpaste cap has not been put on properly or whether the light switch has been left on. All you remember after forty-five minutes, is that you're right, and all that you notice is this purple, throbbing vein on the side of your neck, and you hear yourself saying, "And your *mother*. . .!"

Well, the same scenario often occurs with a salesperson. Even if you know the approach you plan to take, it is all too easy to go off-track. You have to step back and say to yourself, "Just improvising this meeting hasn't really gotten me the best results with this person. I may not be able to help her unless I practice a little." (This is especially true in those situations in which you have ignored the whole process of having a coaching meeting until a crisis or problem arises. This results in the salesperson associating meetings with trauma.)

So, what we need to do is actually practice the approach. To map it out, think about it, and practice our opening question or statement aloud. We have to set up for ourselves how the meeting is going to open, how it is going to move forward, and how we want it to conclude. We are not talking about a particularly long meeting here, but we do have to know the roadmap pretty well.

Plan the meeting, practice it, and adjust your plan depending on the actual human being you will be talking to. Is this salesperson a Yes-Person? Is this person defensive? Your approach will be different based on who you're talking to.

Another set of considerations is the person's board formation and overall performance level. Is the person at expectation? Below expectation? Above expectation? How would you rate this person's performance over the past three months? What is this person's history?

What is this person's likely performance level one month from now if nothing changes? Two months from now? Three months from now?

All these things are going to matter.

In addition, you want to think about specific personality traits that will help motivate him or her in a positive and constructive way.

If you remember nothing else from this portion of the book, I hope you remember this. How you open the meeting will have a dramatic impact on how well the meeting goes—so practice your opening, say it aloud at some point, and map out, on paper, the ideal progression of the coaching meeting you are planning for this person.

#2: Get to the Point!

Once you start the one-on-one coaching meeting, *get to the point*. Again, this is easier to do if you hold the meetings regularly.

If you have the meetings every three months, it's *harder* to get to the point. Things move more slowly, because you haven't built up a rhythm. You are not sure what the protocols are supposed to be, and neither is the salesperson who is probably still worried about whether something terrible is going to happen during the meeting.

Think of the example of a batting coach. The batting coach interacts with the people he has to coach *regularly*. He does not start the discussion from a million miles away. He does not say things like, "You know, hitting is not what I really need to talk to you about. I have to talk to you about the imagery Shakespeare uses in *The Winter's Tale* to describe the process of rebirth, because there are some elaborate examples of imagery from that play that connect to what you have to do in the batter's box."

No, most hitting coaches get right to the point. They say, "This is exactly like the problems that Don Mattingly had when he was in a slump in 1981—and here's how he fixed it. He got a little bit closer up to the plate and changed his hands slightly as he was holding the bat like this. You might want to give that a try."

Again, that's easier to do if the coach sees the guy every day. If he makes a regular habit of initiating these kinds of discussions, he is less likely to get a bad reaction from the batter: "Who the hell are you? Where have you been all season? Who are you to give *me* advice?"

#3: Talk about Ratios

Whether or not you decide to show the salesperson the fifteen-point coaching scale assessment you have completed, you **should be ready to ask about specific ratios:** "How many dials did you make today? How many completed calls? How many appointments did you set?"

1. **Track the ratio of dials to completed calls over time.** This number should emerge as 2:1 or lower. If your people are having problems with this ratio, find out whom they're trying to reach within the target organization. They may not be asking for the right person or title.

2. **Track the ratio of completed calls to appointments over time.** This number should eventually emerge as 3:1 or lower. If your people are having trouble with this ratio, listen in on their calls. They may not be asking directly for the appointment by suggesting a specific date and time.

3. **Monitor the average length of prospecting calls.** If one of your people is routinely spending more than two and a half minutes on prospecting calls, the odds are good that he or she is wasting time by arguing with the prospect. Specifically, during the coaching meeting, you should encourage the salesperson to make three attempts to turn around initial negative responses during prospecting calls—and then to move on!

#4: Stay Away from Words That Make People Freeze Up

Some words and phrases are almost guaranteed to get your sales meeting off to a bad start. Give yourself—and your salesperson—a break by choosing less emotionally loaded phrases.

Here are some examples.

Do Say	Don't Say
Let's . . .	You've got to . . .
Here's what I can do.	That's company policy.
I can . . .	I can't . . .
I'm sorry you feel that way.	You're over-reacting.
Let's find out.	I have no idea.
Can we table that for now?	That's ridiculous.
There must be a way to . . .	You will have to figure that out yourself.
What if next time, you . . .	You should have . . .
And . . .	But . . .
I want to work with you on x. . .	If you don't do x, there will be trouble.
There is only one option I can see.	You have left me with only one alternative.

Coaching Meeting Prep Sheet

Use the worksheet on the following page to prepare for a coaching meeting with an individual salesperson.

Here a few key points to remember when preparing for a coaching session:

- Make sound prospecting habits, including role-plays, part of the routine.
- During role-plays, make sure salespeople understand that they will almost certainly be interrupted when they make cold calls. Help them learn to use their approach to get negative responses out on the table.

And here are a few questions for you, the manager:

- What new ratio-related goals will you set for this person?
- What are the associated skills related to attaining these goals?
- What will your follow-through and mentoring plan be in this area?
- What new growth and development goals will you set for this person?
- What are the associated skills related to attaining these goals?

Name of this sales representative: _____

How long has he/she been with the company?: _____

What is his/her personality type?
(Examples: Boxer, Riddler, Yes-Person, etc.): _____

How would you describe this person's performance over the past three months (at
quota, above quota, below quota)?: _____

_____

_____

Right now, what are this person's two most important performance challenges?
(Possible answers: won't track ratios, discounts too easily, shallow interviewing style,
low average sale figure, consistent failure to hit quota, prospects inconsistently, poor
planning skills): _____

_____

_____

_____

_____

_____

In the space below, please show what this person's relevant prospect totals look like
right now.

_____

_____

_____

_____

_____

_____

_____

_____

_____

How many scheduled first appointments?: _____

How many next steps in place to gain more information? (25%): _____

**How many presentations to the right person with right presentation,
right $, right timetable? (50%):** _____

How many verbal agreements to buy? (90%): _____

How many closed sales? (100%): _____

The Other Side of Coaching: Catch Them in the Act of Doing the Right Stuff

In previous chapters, I've shared the specific areas in which you as a manager have to be willing to take the initiative, execute a battle plan, and take positive action to change what is actually happening on the ground in the world your sales team inhabits.

As important as those steps are, however, I want to emphasize that this should not be your only philosophy for instilling positive change. There is another, passive side to coaching, a particularly important side that sales managers all too often ignore. This is "the art of catching people doing the right stuff." I am certainly not the first person to call attention to this important part of the manager's job description.

Many of us were once successful salespeople, and we are well acquainted—or should be—with the importance of setting up a to-do list and taking action on it. However, the simple act of observing, noticing, and praising somebody effusively when they get something right makes just as much difference as correcting a "fault," and probably more.

This process is a little subtler, however, and it is frequently forgotten in the hustle and bustle of the average selling day. In the following sections, keep an eye out for certain easy-to-miss behaviors in specific areas—behaviors that your team members may well get right on their own. When that happens, find the right setting to praise and reward those particular actions.

Catch Them in the Act of Thinking about the Team First

"Me, me, me"—to hear some people talk, that's all salespeople focus on.

The reality is a little different. There are certainly going to be members of your team who buy into your company's vision and make a point of sacrificing their own interests in order to accomplish something important for the group as a whole. Sometimes a team member will even back off on a smaller deal so that a larger one can happen, even though she won't be getting a commission on the larger deal. When that kind of thing happens, make a point of noticing it.

If you can reinforce this trait in one or more people, you'll instill a sense of purpose and keep the team focused on the rewards associated with working together harmoniously.

Catch Them in the Act of Accepting Personal Responsibility

Imagine a whole team full of salespeople who commit to taking personal responsibility for their own results. Imagine a world where salespeople who forget to stay in touch with a key contact admit that's what happened, rather than concocting some lame story about the person being unavailable for eleven straight weeks. Imagine a world where nobody on the sales staff whines about not getting enough support, or enough information, or enough lead-time, or enough help from Operations.

Okay, I admit that's a lot to imagine. The point remains, however, that sales managers who get tired of whining have a duty to praise and reward salespeople when they actually do sit up and accept responsibility for what they do. Make sure you acknowledge and appreciate every situation in which a salesperson says, "Yep, I did that, and I'm responsible for what happened as a result." (Even if that means overlooking, for just a moment, the mistake or the situation that the person is taking responsibility for.)

If you can reinforce this trait in one or more people, you'll give salespeople who might otherwise be inclined to whine endlessly a different model of behavior to consider.

Catch Them in the Act of Training Less Experienced Team Members (Whether Formally or Informally)

Some of your more experienced salespeople will interact well with people who don't know quite as much about the job as they do. If you agree with the lessons they're passing along, encourage these people, either in public or in private (your call).

These salespeople will spontaneously offer encouragement and explanation to junior team members who need help. They enjoy inspiring others and may see the "elder statesman" role (whatever their age) as a vehicle for attaining status within the organization. As long as the experience they bring to the table is relevant and the conclusions they draw from past mistakes more or less match your philosophy, thank them for their efforts.

If you can reinforce this trait in one or more people, you'll make adjustment and growth a great deal easier for the less experienced members of your team, and you'll deliver higher job satisfaction to someone whose experience and guidance is worthy of recognition. (The senior member of the team who likes offering advice may or may not be looking for a career path into management. Sometimes actual bottom-line responsibility for a group's sales totals is a little more reality than anybody ordered. But we could have told them that.)

Catch Them in the Act of Making an Effort to Understand the Viewpoints of Others

Some salespeople live to fight with their managers. Whatever the issue, the manager is wrong, and they're right.

As a sales manager, you may eventually find yourself in a dispute over something or other with this kind of salesperson. Do yourself a favor. Keep an eye out for some situation—any situation—*that lies outside of the context of your most recent disagreement* and that demonstrates this person's ability to see things from someone else's point of view. Then praise that person to the heavens for his or her ability to walk a mile in someone else's shoes.

If you can reinforce this trait in one or more people, you'll have fewer conflicts with salespeople who insist that they're right and you're wrong, even if they've forgotten what it is that they were supposed to be arguing about.

Coaching Scenarios

How would you plan your next coaching meeting, based on the following scenarios?

Activity Report: Marvin Smith

Marvin has been with you for six months; he could be described as a top performer. His Prospect Management Board now reflects some big deals at 50 percent and 90 percent, but a disturbing lack of first appointments.

- Marvin does not think that having a schedule for the day adds any real value. He would rather operate without one. His reasoning is that there's too much paperwork involved in preparing a daily schedule—paperwork that is taking him away from his customers. He prefers to "improvise" and "address problems as they come up."

- You have noticed recently that although Marvin has been a top performer, his total visits have been slowly declining over the past two months.

- Today, one of Marvin's 50 percent prospects closed.

What would your objective be for the next coaching meeting with Marvin?
How would you open the meeting?
What Next Step would you like to set with Marvin after the meeting?
What should he have done by that point?

Activity Report: Juan Martinez

Juan has been with you for three years; he could be described as an average performer. His Prospect Management Board is relatively well balanced, but his total dollar value seems low to you.

Juan's personality style is that of the Know-It-All.

- Juan thinks that the deals he is not winning are related to internal obstacles.

- Juan goes on plenty of appointments with new prospects—more than his target, in fact—but his ability to generate revenue from his penetrated base seems below average to you.

- Juan is supportive of, and helpful toward, less-experienced team members. He has mentioned several times that he feels he has the potential to be "a team leader."

What would your objective be for the next coaching meeting with Juan?
How would you open the meeting?
What Next Step would you like to set with Juan after the meeting?
What should he have done by that point?

Activity Report: Mike Jones

Mike has been with you for three months; so far, he could be described as a struggling performer. His Prospect Management Board reflects a great deal of wishful thinking and little meaningful activity. Very little of his activity actually moves forward to 25 percent—although Mike frequently attempts to place leads in that column that actually have no Next Step attached to them.

Mike's personality style is Me Now. He often seems to have a short attention span. You have doubts about his time management skills.

- Mike is in the middle of a series of meetings with a large customer.

- He tells you that he is facing heavy competitive pressure on pricing from this customer. He is at a loss about what to do next.

- Mike stayed late today to work on an "important proposal" for a meeting tomorrow.

What would your objective be for the next coaching meeting with Mike?
How would you open the meeting?
What Next Step would you like to set with Mike after the meeting?
What should he have done by that point?

Activity Report: June Reed

June has been with you for four years; she was once a high-level performer on your team but is having a difficult year. Her Prospect Management Board does not look good; it is particularly low on 50 percent and 90 percent entries. She has not come close to hitting her targets for new business.

June's personality style is that of the Boxer.

- June's target is to go on an average of four visits a day.

- In practice, her number is just under three visits a day over the past three months.

- Recently, you asked about June's last six meetings and were dismayed at what you heard. She doesn't seem to be calling on the right people, and she is selling too low in the target organization. You also get the feeling that she is not effectively targeting current customers as prospects for future business.

What would your objective be for the next coaching meeting with June?
How would you open the meeting?
What Next Step would you like to set with June after the meeting?
What should she have done by that point?

People are complex beings, and we have to practice interacting with them.

There are no right answers for those scenarios—only opportunities for you to brainstorm and set priorities.

Worksheets and Forms You Can Use for the Coaching Meeting

On the following pages, you will find reproductions of some forms we have used successfully in helping sales managers and the members of their sales teams track specific, measurable change in their daily activities. If these forms, or some adaptation of them, are helpful to you in establishing rapport with your salesperson during the coaching meetings, assign them as prework.

Some abbreviations to know:

D stands for *Dials*

CC stands for *Completed Calls* with someone who could give us an appointment.

A stands for *Scheduled First Appointment*.

V stands for *Total Face-to-Face Visits*.

S stands for *Sales*.

Integrated Coaching System Log		GLOSSARY -- Dial: Call to a lead you have not called for 5 business days. Completed Call: Discussion with someone you'd like to meet with for the first time. First Appointment: Scheduled meeting with someone who has agreed to meet with you for the first time. Visit: Actual face-to-face meeting with a prospect (either initial meeting or follow-through meeting). Prospect: Someone who meets with you for a second time.	
SALESPERSON COMPLETES THIS UNSHADED SECTION		**MANAGER COMPLETES THIS SHADED SECTION**	
A. My commission-driven income goal for last quarter:		Does this figure match your expectations/quota?	
B. My average commission per sale:		Is this figure accurate?	
C. Sales required last quarter to attain the goal in A. (Divide "A" by "B")		Is the salesperson's assessment accurate?	
D. Sales I actually did close last quarter:		Is the salesperson's assessment accurate? If so, EVALUATE THIS FIGURE as Below Expectation, Above Expectation, or At Expectation.	Below Expectation At Expectation Above Expectation
E. My commission-driven income goal for today to the end of the fiscal year:		Does this figure match your expectations/quota?	
F. Total number of sales I must close in order to attain this goal. (Divide "E" by "B")		Does this figure match your expectations/quota?	
G. Total number of *Dials* I must make to generate a single First Appointment. (Review your activity for the past 90 days to determine a *realistic* number.)		Does this figure match your expectations/quota?	
H. Total number of *First Appointments* I must set in order to generate a single active prospect. (Review your activity for the past 90 days to determine a *realistic* number.)		Does this figure match your expectations/quota?	
I. *Active Prospects* I need in order to generate a single sale. (Review your activity for the past 90 days to determine a *realistic* number.)		Does this figure match your expectations/quota?	
J. TOTAL *Active Prospects* I must generate between now and the end of the fiscal year to hit my income goal. (Multiply "I" by "F")		Does this figure match your expectations/quota?	
K. TOTAL *First Appointments* I must set to generate that many prospects between now and the end of the fiscal year. (Multiply "J" by "H")		Does this figure match your expectations/quota?	
L. TOTAL *Dials* I must make to generate that many first appointments. (Multiply "K" by "G")		Does this figure match your expectations/quota?	
M. Working days between now and the end of the fiscal year.		Does this figure match your expectations/quota?	
N. DAILY QUOTA of dials per day needed to hit my income goal. (Divide "L" by "M")		Does this figure match your expectations/quota?	

My Daily Dial Quota:

_____

Signed

_____

You can use the Manager's Change Log to track the areas of ongoing improvement you are monitoring for each team member.

Integrated Coaching System Checklist: Manager's Change Log

SALESPERSON:_____
Date of coaching session_____

Below Expectation	At Expectation	Above Expectation	Skills and Capabilities	Comments
			Prospecting	
			Cold calling	
			Rapport development	
			Eye contact/ Non-verbal signals	
			Transition to interviewing	
			Identifying key information	
			Verifying information	
			Product malleability (Shaping for the client)	
			Presentation	
			Handling/solving objections	
			Closing techniques	
			Cross selling	
			Follow-up	

Short term goals for this salesperson: | (Coaching priority: High, Medium, Low)

Next scheduled coaching date: 4/01/03

Long-Term Performance Worksheet for Salesperson

Yearly Overview to be completed by salesperson:

Your Name _____

A. Last year's actual dollar volume: _____

B. Total number of accounts in your base last year: _____

C. Average value per account last year (*A* divided by *B*): _____

D. Total value of new accounts last year: _____

E. Total number of new accounts last year: _____

F. Average value of a new account (*D* divided by *E*): _____

G. Number of *first appointments* you set last year (est.): _____

Long-Term Performance Worksheet for Manager

Salesperson's Name _____

You will need the salesperson's completed Yearly Overview *to complete this form. (Note: double-check the salesperson's figures for accuracy and validity of estimates.)*

1. Last year's base of business ($): _____

2. This year's total quota ($): _____

3. Average value per account last year (see line C of salesperson's worksheet): _____

4. Average value per new account last year (see line F of salesperson's worksheet): _____

5. Difference between this year's total quota (line 2) and last year's base of business (line 1): _____

6. Total number of new accounts necessary to hit this year's quota (line 5 divided by line 4): _____

7. Total number of first appointments set last year (see line G of salesperson's worksheet): _____

8. Total number of new accounts last year (see line E of salesperson's worksheet): _____

9. Number of first appointments necessary to develop a single new account (line 7 divided by line 8): _____

10. Total first appointments needed between now and end of year to develop target number of new accounts (line 9 multiplied by line 6): _____

Weekly Coaching Meeting "Talk Sheet" (for Salesperson)

Name:

Date:

My biggest challenge this week was:

My current #1 prospect:

Date and time of next contact with this prospect:

This week, the main thing I plan to do differently is:

Here's what I need help on:

Mentor's input/Goal for next session:

Weekly Tracking Sheet
(for Manager—Use with Weekly Coaching Meeting "Talk Sheet")

Name:	Date:

Ratios for last week: D: CC: A: V: S:	Last week's board formation (list current totals in these categories): 25 50 90

Ratios for year to date: D: CC: A: V: S:	This week's board formation (list current totals in these categories): 25 50 90

Person's current #1 prospect:	Date and time of next scheduled contact with this prospect:

Current strengths:

Current weaknesses:

This week, the main thing for this person to do differently is:

Areas where this person may need help from others in the organization this week are:

Mentor's notes:

What I planned for us to discuss:

What we actually discussed:

Goal for next mentoring session:

Working with the Team: The Eight-Week Coaching Plan

In this book, I've repeatedly stressed the importance of having an ongoing coaching program. That's just as important to do on the group level, as it is to do with individual salespeople. Effective ongoing follow-through is essential to any coaching plan.

To launch your coaching program for the group, call the team together for a brief meeting. You should, of course, prepare what you're going to say ahead of time; use the following bullets as starting points for a short written outline.

- *Why I'm calling this meeting.* There has to be some purpose for the gathering *other than* "You people are not hitting the mark." If you like, use the fact that you've read this book as an excuse to change or formalize the group coaching routine. Other good reasons include: "My boss made me call this meeting." "I recently completed a training program that inspired me to call this meeting." "Competitive challenge *x* inspired me to call this meeting."

- *Where I think we are now.* Give your best assessment of the competitive situation your company/team faces. Give your best assessment of the group's biggest asset as a team. Give your best assessment of the areas in which you think improvement is necessary.

- *Where I'd like to see us twelve months from now.* Outline the team's long-term goal. Explain why you think it's important. Connect it to something positive (like a team bonus) that everyone can understand.

- *Where I'd like to see us eight weeks from now.* Identify an eight-week goal that supports the one-year goal. Then lay out the plan for your next eight weeks of group coaching.

What should that plan look like? Read on.

A Rotating Program

To follow this program properly, institute a series of weekly coaching events, developed in rotating eight-week outlines. The team-coaching program should never stop.

This approach allows your team to receive consistent feedback on critical goals and helps inspire everybody who works for you. It's proof that you're willing to commit to the sales staff as a group and as individuals.

> Nothing you or anyone else can train an individual, or a sales staff, to do will stick—unless you reinforce it over time.

When coaching is an ongoing part of the sales management process, team members are more likely to "buy in" and support coaching goals. If there is no ongoing plan, then the organization is likely to be perceived as having no direction.

Inspiring salespeople means persuading them to follow your company's lead with enthusiasm, but it's hard to get people to follow you if they don't know where you're going!

The Eight-Week Coaching Plan: A Sample Outline

In the following sections, you will find a sample outline for your eight-week coaching plan. Use these chapters as an outline for your own plan. As part of my consulting work with managers, I have successfully implemented this format in just about any industry you can imagine.

Week 1: Team Meeting/Overview

Preview the fact that regular one-on-one and team-coaching meetings will begin next week. Set up a coaching schedule with lots of short sessions that will happen one-on-one with all team members.

Discuss the relevant short- and long-term goals with the group. Specifically, identify the goal you want the team to achieve at the conclusion of this eight-week plan. (Use what you've learned about the group from completing the Fifteen Coaching Points checklist.)

> Team goals and individual goals should be "makeable." This is particularly important for the first goal you set. People tend to believe that they *cannot* change, and we want to give them evidence to the contrary in the first couple of weeks of the eight-week plan.

Identify exactly what's going to be monitored. (Daily calls? Daily first appointments? Visits in the field? Total value of all closed business for the week? All of these?)

I strongly suggest that you introduce the Prospect Management System at this meeting, if you have not done so already, and explain how you will be helping people to implement it.

Assign activities for next week's meetings. Let people know that you will be conducting the Role Discrepancy Exercise (Chapter 19) with each individual sales representative. Assign the exercise before the one-on-one meeting; during the one-on-one meeting, you will compare your version of the exercise to the salesperson's version, and discuss the differences.

In addition, you can ask each individual salesperson to prepare for the one-on-one coaching meeting by writing one-sentence answers to the following questions:

- What is my greatest strength as a salesperson?

- What is my greatest weakness as a salesperson?

- What key changes should I make that will help the team hit the eight-week goal?

Get ready for next week's meetings by writing down *your* answers to the same three questions for the salesperson.

Week 2: Start the One-on-One Meetings

Conduct the first coaching session with each of the individual salespeople. As part of that, negotiate which specific measurable areas you're going to work on improving with this salesperson over the next seven weeks. (Use what you've learned from completing the Fifteen Coaching Points checklist.)

Important: By this point, you should be collecting the information you said you'd collect in Week 1.

Week 3: Dynamic

A Dynamic is a contest, game, or event—something that shakes people up.

Example: Everyone who sets two appointments a day for the week wins a prize.

You can also announce the *winner* of the contest without announcing the terms of the contest! ("You didn't know it, but this week there was a contest for total dials. Because Joe made the most total dials this week, he wins a $50 gift certificate to Blockbuster.")

This could also be a non-contest-related group event (like a team dinner). Whatever you choose as your Dynamic, it should reinforce and reward, directly or indirectly, the activities that support your team's eight-week goal.

Continue the weekly one-on-one coaching meetings you set up in Week 1.

Week 4: Halfway Evaluation

Call a team meeting. Discuss the group's progress so far. Be enthusiastic, but remember that enthusiasm alone is not what the coaching plan is about. How is the campaign going? What are the benchmarks telling you?

Focus on *measurable* activities (dials, first appointments, Next Steps).

Celebrate and acknowledge group or individual progress toward the goal you established for the team.

Continue the weekly one-on-one coaching meetings you set up in Week 1.

Week 5: Training

Target this to the specific areas of improvement you want to encourage, *based on the results of your assessment of the group, and the halfway evaluation.*

Use resources like books, tapes, or other internal training resources. You might, for instance, encourage senior sales representatives to share their insights with the team.

Another interesting approach is to pick the *weakest* person in a certain skill area and hold him or her accountable for the training session. This is not as strange an idea as it sounds. Pick (for instance) the person who currently has the *lowest* level of success at cold calling. Assign this person to read the book *Cold Calling Techniques (That Really Work!)*, and then summarize the key points from the book for the entire group during a half-hour or hour-long training session in Week 5.

The following resources, included in the appendix of this book, can support your training efforts in Week 5:

1. Fifteen Critical Selling Principles (page 233)

2. Three Principles for Effective Time Management (page 245)

3. The Next Step: An Overview (page 237)

4. The Nine Principles of Cold Calling (page 235)

5. Sixteen Ways to Ask for a Next Step (page 240)

Continue the weekly one-on-one coaching meetings you set up in Week 1.

Week 6: Dynamic, Revisited

Take a new approach to shaking people up.

Use a *different* activity than you used in Week 3.

Surprise the team!

Continue the weekly one-on-one coaching meetings you set up in Week 1.

Week 7: Progress Evaluation and New Goal Discussion

With the team, give your personal assessment of the progress your team has made toward its eight-week goal. How close is the team to pulling it off? What rewards can you offer to make the final push a success?

Continue the weekly one-on-one coaching meetings you set up in Week 1. Repeat the strengths and weaknesses exercise you did in Week 2. What has changed?

Week 8: Reassess

Conduct a group evaluation/discussion of the final numbers. Get feedback from team members on what worked and what didn't. Preview the next eight-week plan, and start the cycle again next week!

Note: Senior managers should monitor the ongoing eight-week plan objectives. Do the goals in question match *your* goals for this group? What does the eight-week plan look like for *each* sales manager who reports to you? Are your managers focusing on the skills you want to see improved? Are they likely to result in the outcomes you're hoping to achieve?

What We Figured Out in This Section

- The human side of the coaching equation is more difficult than the strategic side.

- Pay close attention to salespeople over a long period; find reasons to praise them, and work with them to identify goals that will inspire them to fulfill your vision of the job.

- The Fifteen Coaching Points help you to categorize, identify, and coach three groups of salespeople: Level One, Level Two, and Level Three.

- This system will also help you forecast income from your team accurately.

- Members of each of the three groups are likely to have distinct challenges.

- Certain challenges, however, can happen to *any* salesperson; the Prospect Management System will help you coach improvements to these challenges.

- Effective coaching requires skills in:

  - Motivation

  - Communication

  - Training

  - One-on-one coaching sessions

- Salespeople have certain personality patterns; if you know what they are, you can do a better job of coaching them.

- Ongoing reinforcement is essential; set up, and repeat, an Eight-Week Coaching Plan with your team.

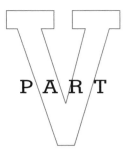

Hiring—
and Keeping Together—
the #1 Sales Team

So far, we've been talking about how you can manage and motivate a top-flight sales team. But how can you tell if someone would make a great addition to the team? And how can you hold onto your most successful salespeople? That's what this section is all about.

Hiring a #1 Sales Team: Do's

There are, I suppose, as many theories about how to hire a great sales team as there are sales managers. The following principles and guidelines are offered, not as the last word on a subject that deserves a book of its own, but rather as an overview of what has actually worked for me over the years. If it's helpful to you, use any or all of it. If any advice here contradicts something that's already working for you, just ignore it.

The advice I'm passing along, for better or worse, in this chapter and the following falls into two categories: dos and don'ts. If you review both halves carefully, you will, at the very least, be able to implement the strategies we've used at my company over the past quarter century to avoid the most common mistakes when it comes to hiring salespeople.

Do: Identify the most common factors for sales success on your team.

Do you know what your ideal performer looks like?

Before you begin to address the question, "Whom should I hire?" ask yourself the related question, "Whom among my current team members would I most like to *retain*—and what do those people have in common?" Obviously, this question is not very useful if you are starting from scratch or have no successful performers on staff. But in the more common scenario where you have at least one or two people who are implementing best practices, it makes sense to attempt to create a list of what those people are actually doing right. Then recruit with those factors in mind. A good starting point would be the Fifteen Coaching Points checklist, which you will find on page 253.

Once you have completed that form for your most productive salespeople, you will have a good idea of the activities and profiles you should be looking for in your next hire. Consider going even further by identifying company-specific and industry-specific skills that you may be able to look for in recruits. For instance, if your team is focused on advertising sales, knowledge of the advertising industry—specifically the necessity of working with advertising agencies—is going to be an important job-related factor. Try to write down at least ten key skill areas or personal history elements that you would like to see in your next hire, and make sure these are based on actual performance and experience traits in the current team.

Earlier, I mentioned the 80/20 maxim, that 20 percent of the sales force provides 80 percent of the income from the sales team as a whole. Your job, as a manager, is to discover exactly what that 20 percent looks like. What do people in that group have in common? How should the traits that they share affect your recruiting goals?

It is highly likely that top sales performers in your organization share traits like an ability to engage strangers in a conversation, but what other traits do they possess? Analytical ability? Specific software skills? Knowledge of marketing and demographic issues? Whatever those skills are, it is your job to identify those traits—and then use the information to your advantage in your recruiting campaign.

Before you do anything else, take a good, long look at your industry, your organization, and the top people on your staff. Find out what commonalities exist among those team members who have been meeting or preferably exceeding quota for a sustained period. If you wish, you can begin the process by identifying the people you would most like to retain on a staff. Who could you least afford to lose? How big is that group? What key selling traits do they share? What do they do that other salespeople don't? Make that list and then use it to drive your interviews with the salespeople who want to join your team.

Do: Create a formal job description.

If you do not already have one, write one. If you do already have one, you should probably consider revising it to match the skill capabilities you identified in the previous exercise.

Identify the compensation structure you are currently offering, and ask yourself if it needs changing. This is not always easy, but it is incredibly important, because different salespeople require different compensation packages.

Do: Identify whether you are looking for mentors or young guns.

Mentors are supposed to help other people learn. Young guns are supposed to build their own careers. Decide what you want. It's highly unlikely, in my experience at least, for an organization to be searching for both kinds of salespeople at the same time. The company is usually either searching for one type (because it has too many of the other) or trying to get the two groups to talk to each other. A wise man once said, "Even the biggest dog was once a pup." During any given hiring campaign, you are likely to be looking to supplement your team of big dogs—or looking to supplement your team of pups. Know which goal you're trying to attain and bear in mind the strengths and weaknesses of each group, as shown in the following table:

Veterans		Newcomers	
Assets	Liabilities	Assets	Liabilities
Industry knowledge and experience. Previous sales experience. Existing contacts. More experience in internal politics.	May have already plateaued or be about to plateau. May cop an attitude, especially when you try to get them to prospect regularly. May have become cynical/jaded. More experience in internal politics.	Don't know what they can't do. May have high energy and enthusiasm. May be easier to get them to prospect regularly. Less experience in internal politics.	Lack of experience in complex deals. May make major interviewing and "deal structure" mistakes. Projections/ expectations often surrealistically wrong. Less experience in internal politics.

Do: Conduct an effective interview.

See Chapter 76 for specific interview questions that are part of successful interviews.

Hiring a #1 Sales Team: Don'ts

The following are some of the pitfalls you may encounter in hiring your team.

Don't: Fall victim to the "halo effect."

In this all-too-familiar syndrome, managers are distracted by surface considerations in an applicant; that is, superficial resemblances to other hires who have worked out well. In other words, if your top salesperson has blond hair, reads a lot of science fiction, and stands six feet six inches tall, another applicant who shares those three traits may lead you, consciously or unconsciously, to believe that the same likelihood for success exists. Big mistake. Remember that each individual applicant is just that—an individual.

I prefer to make applicants who bear certain surface resemblances to successful salespeople on my staff work *harder* than the average applicant to get the job offer. If the person seems "just like Bill Quotabeater," that should be no problem, right?

Don't: Hire people who squirm in social situations.

The advice I just gave you about avoiding superficial resemblances is important, but one "superficial" trait is usually a high predictor of success among sales applicants: an outgoing personality.

Of course, it is *possible* for someone to put together a successful sales career despite a habitual unwillingness to deal with others in face-to-face social situations, but it sure is difficult. (And I'm willing to bet it's exceedingly rare.) When you interview someone for a sales job, you are interviewing, not merely to analyze the person's wording in answering your questions, but also the person's ability to handle himself or herself comfortably in a business setting. The person should *enjoy* shaking hands and making eye contact. The person should *enjoy* talking to you. The person should *enjoy* fielding a tough question.

To a very large degree, the way the salesperson works with you during the interview is a predictable indicator of the way he or she will represent your company to a prospect during a sales meeting. If you spot constant stammering, serious signs of nervousness, or perpetual inconsistency in answers to important questions, you should probably think twice before offering this person the sales job.

Some managers go out of their way to discount the negative implications of a jittery job interview, on the theory that "a job interview is a stressful situation." I sometimes feel like asking those managers: "Suppose you want this salesperson to close a big deal for you. Suppose your team's yearly quota is based on how this person performs during a single meeting with a big prospect. Do you imagine that *won't* be a stressful situation?"

Don't: Do all the work for them.

It is important not to make the hiring process too easy for a salesperson. Let's face it, the dynamic here is just a little bit different if you were hiring someone to answer phones, take messages, and photocopy documents. You're trying to determine whether this person is capable of running a sales meeting. Why not throw in a couple of awkward silences during the job interview, just to see what happens?

You can (and should, in my view) take this principle even further. One of my pet peeves, for example, is an applicant for a sales job who refuses to do any research on my company or to ask me any intelligent questions. After the interview, if I say, "Do you have any questions for me?" and the person instantly says, "Nope," that's a problem. Now, if I were to hire this person to represent my company in meetings with senior corporate leaders, I would expect her to find out a little bit about the organization she's meeting with before walking in the door. I would expect her to prepare some intelligent, specific questions for that decision-maker. That's why I want to hear a salesperson say: "Yes, I do have a question for you. Why are you hiring salespeople right now?" Why wouldn't she want to know that?

I'll give you another example of this same "don't do all the work for them" principle in action: Sometimes, to test a promising candidate, I will conclude the interview without telling the salesperson what's going to happen next. I want to see if he will ask directly what has to happen for him to get the job.

I've found that leaving the status of the salesperson's application in doubt at the end of the meeting is an excellent way to gauge his willingness to take the initiative necessary to move things forward in the sales cycle. Faced with this situation, I've found that a superior sales applicant will *always* try to quantify exactly where he is in the process. This person will try to find out how salespeople have been hired in the past, and what he needs to do to move forward. (This "where do I stand" dilemma is, of course, a very good analogue to the hazy status many prospects try to leave in place at the end of a sales meeting.)

Another interesting question, assuming you have four or five qualified candidates, is this one: Which of these people will do the best job of following up with you *after* the interview?

Here's the bottom line: People who take charge of meetings (tactfully, of course) tend to do very well in business in general, and sales in particular. Consider the job interview just such a meeting. Test the person. Look for signs that she is capable of excelling at the game of social tennis that is selling.

Specific Interview Questions

What follows are some of my favorite questions for use during job interviews with salespeople. I've included the questions, some commentary on what the questions are intended to elucidate, and my own suggestions regarding the kind of answers you should want.

Tell me a little bit about yourself. You're looking for two things here: some meaningful background information, and the applicant's willingness and ability to tailor that background to suit a particular situation. Right now, whether he realizes it or not, the applicant is in fact a salesperson. He is selling the product/service known as "My Candidacy." You can gain some insight on the strategies this person would use to portray your company in the best possible light by examining the strategies he uses to put past experiences in the best possible light. Danger signs would be blatant exaggerations or falsehoods (if you can pick up on them, so will a prospect) or the opposite problem—a boring recitation of past events that has no connection whatsoever with the work profile.

How has your experience in (college, community college, whatever the person was doing before this) prepared you to sell for this company? Keep an ear out for examples of persuasive ability. These may or may not be directly related to activities that have clear parallels with sales activities (like fundraising, marketing plan development, or direct mail design). In addition to these obviously relevant anecdotes, note any experience that spotlights the applicant's ability to set goals and get what she wants. If this person won a special exemption to a rule against midnight concerts, for instance, after having booked a popular band for a post-final-exam bash, that demonstrates an ability to make a case, deliver a presentation, and "close the deal" by means of discussions with influential people. Independently arranged travel and internships may also be worth exploring.

What made you decide to apply to this company for this job? What you're not looking for: A vacant stare and a shrug of the shoulders, followed by mumbling along the lines of, "You put an ad in the paper, and I answered it." Instead, you're hoping to get evidence that this person has some basic idea of what your company does, to whom it sells, and why selling your product/service to that group of people is the most interesting professional challenge on the horizon. Sure, you both know that the person is interviewing at other companies—but you want to see some evidence that this person can show the appropriate signs of being "on a mission" and enjoying it. That means offering compelling *reasons* for doing what he is doing right now. If you don't get a story or detail that conveys genuine enthusiasm, beware: A similarly sluggish response may be forthcoming during a sales meeting when the *prospect* says, "Tell me why you decided to work for this company."

What do you think it takes to be a successful salesperson? Not, as some managers imagine, a question designed solely for the veteran applicant. Someone applying for her first sales position should also be able to come up with a convincing answer and explain the reasoning behind it. Just about any brief response can and should be explored with this follow-up: "What makes you say that?" Give extra points for answers that acknowledge the importance of prospecting and information gathering. Consider hiring on the spot if the person prefaces any discussion of negotiation or closing skills with a reminder that these two activities are impossible if the prospect isn't interacting with the salesperson, and assuming half of the responsibility for the development of the proposal.

Give me a specific example of a time you faced a tough problem and dealt with it effectively. This is a classic "what's-this-person-really-made-of" question. You're looking for a story that provides evidence of intelligence, diplomacy, and an ability to respond quickly and constructively to unexpected challenges. The details of the story should, of course, be something that a current or past supervisor would verify, although you do have an obvious tact requirement in the case of an applicant who passes along a success story that connects to a current employer.

(Just for good measure, you might ask the applicant to supply another example that comes from an employment stint at a company where he is not currently working.) Last but not least, and I don't know why sales managers so frequently forget this, you're looking for evidence that the applicant knows how to deliver a compelling verbal account of a past triumph. If he stutters and stammers through an anecdote you can barely understand, that's no endorsement of his selling ability.

Tell me why you think you have what it takes to succeed here. There are, to my way of thinking, two good answers to this. The first can be summarized as follows: "I'm the kind of person who has what it takes to succeed anywhere, and your company is no exception." This viewpoint is, of course, a common working assumption for most successful salespeople, so if you hear this answer delivered confidently, plus examples to back it up, that's a good thing. The other good answer to this question sounds like this: "Well, based on what little I've heard about your company, I'm pretty sure I'd do well here, but I'm not going to pretend I know enough about this job to be able to tell you exactly why I'm going to be successful here. Frankly, there are still many things I don't know. So can I ask you a couple of questions about the job?" As a general but reliable rule, I make a point of hiring salespeople who aren't afraid to ask intelligent questions and who don't mind me correcting them—after all, that means they probably won't mind being corrected by prospects.

It's perfectly acceptable to get a hybrid of both answers. For instance: "I think I'm the kind of person who could do well in just about any selling environment, but it sounds to me as though there's something specific about the sales team here that you think new team members should be aware of. I guess I'd have to ask you for some guidance on that. If I were working for you, and I showed up here tomorrow for the first time, what kinds of challenges would you want me to focus on?"

If you had the opportunity to do anything over again, what would you do differently? Only one wrong answer here: "Nothing." Some applicants might be foolhardy enough to believe that a response like that shows just how effective, strong, and decisive they are. Actually, what the question is measuring is a person's ability to step back and think of times when a different approach or a better question would have produced a better result. I'd be looking for a question from the applicant to clarify exactly what I meant. For instance: "You mean in terms of my career, or are you talking about a specific prospect meeting that I wish I had another chance to prepare for?" My personal opinion is that a salesperson (aspiring or veteran) who can't think of a single lesson—from, say, a botched meeting or a call that didn't get returned on time—is not likely to be my kind of salesperson. Such an applicant is misleading you, which means she is likely to tell you tall tales during sales meetings and coaching sessions. (Important note: If you detect signs of discomfort, and get an answer like "Nothing," it's possible that the applicant is thrown by the question, and thinks that's the only safe response. Consider rephrasing the query: "I guess I wasn't being clear. I was really looking for a situation in which you might have made a mistake, and learned something valuable from that experience that you might want to pass on to someone else.")

Have you ever had a disagreement with a manager (or instructor)? If the applicant looks you in the eye and tells you no, you're either dealing with the modern-day equivalent of Mother Teresa or you're being fed a line. Can you guess which is more likely? In the event of a yes answer, follow up with: "Can you tell me a little bit about what happened and how you dealt with it?" A good answer is one that acknowledges that human beings don't always get along, and that the applicant knows how to discuss, negotiate, and disengage from workplace conflicts. A bad answer is one that implies (or states outright) that everything on earth that goes wrong is, ultimately, the boss's fault. You don't really want to hire someone like that, do you?

What makes someone a good team player? This is an important question to ask if you have doubts about this applicant's willingness or ability to support other members of the sales staff—by, for instance, sharing referrals, offering helpful input on proposals, and sharing experiences that seem relevant. Ideally, you're looking for an answer that delivers a story about how the person worked constructively on a deal that did not connect directly to a commission, but benefited the organization as a whole. Of course, you'll want to keep an ear open for signs that the applicant considers team play to be something that is restricted to softball diamonds on Saturday afternoons. It is possible, of course, that the salesperson who thinks this way is a superstar in the making, and you know as well as I do that *some* superstar salespeople have a way of making up their own rules as they go along. Forewarned is forearmed.

Tell me about your numbers. Typically, the salesperson will go off on a tangent about how much money he made last year. That's not what you're after, of course, although it might be interesting to see if the answers match up with what is on the resume. What you are actually asking about here is the person's understanding of his own daily ratios as they connect to sales performance over time. (See the opening chapters of this book for more on this.)

Why are you looking for work now? This one is so obvious most sales managers forget to ask it. It's important to pose this question both to applicants who are currently unemployed and to those who are interviewing while working at another company. The answer should give you some indication of the person's recent employment history and her attitude toward recent employers. If the salesperson offers no meaningful answer, or instantly blames past supervisors for problems on the job, your Spidey sense should start tingling.

What will your references say when I call them? Don't skip this step. Find out what recent sales managers have had to say about this person's performance.

Where do you see yourself going in the next two to three years? It has become a cliché for hiring managers to ask some variation on this question, but it is nevertheless quite important. You need to know what problems in this person's world this job will be solving, and how the position is likely to fit into his personal career plan.

Tell me about a time when you closed a deal nobody thought you would get. An experienced salesperson should have five or six of these kinds of stories, at least. (If you are interviewing someone new to the field of selling, or someone who has very little experience in sales, consider asking the following question instead.)

Give me an example of a time you persuaded someone to do something that you wanted done. This is a good question to ask newcomers to the field of selling. You're looking for evidence that the person in question has (for example) performed telephone solicitations for a favorite charity, or gotten a celebrity to give a speech for a student group.

What do you think of our company? This is a good way to identify exactly how much research the person has done on your firm.

What would you do if I told you I thought your performance here during the interview has been a real problem for me? If you decide to ask this one, ask it politely. The objective here is not to humiliate the salesperson, but rather to get a fix on how he or she responds to stressful exchanges with prospects. Notice that you have not said that the person's performance is sub par, but merely implied it. How will he or she respond to the question: by attacking you in response to a perceived attack, or by asking intelligent questions about what might have gone wrong?

Why should I hire you? This is a good, perhaps indispensable question, and one that any aspiring salesperson should be able to answer with conviction and enthusiasm.

Compensation Plans

It's true that money is not the only source of potential job dissatisfaction among salespeople. It's just as true, though, that poorly designed compensation programs cause some teams to lose contributors they'd like to retain.

Many people have spent a lot of time and effort over the last few decades trying to answer the seemingly simple question: "What is the best payment structure for an individual salesperson?" I don't think anyone has a short, accurate, and reliable answer for that question yet. But there are some generalizations that will apply to certain groups of salespeople, and those generalizations, while not perfect as guidelines for any individual selling team, are something you should be aware of as you craft your own compensation plans.

Any number of compensation plans *could* make a difference, positively or negatively for the people on your team. But the plans all seem to fall into two broad categories. Think of your own compensation plan and ask yourself, "Of these two categories, which comes *closest* to describing our plan?"

1. **All upside, high risk.** This package gives the salesperson an unlimited earning capacity: The company's initial investment guarantee for a particular monthly salary level is minimal.

2. **No risk, low income, low long-term income potential.** This package offers the lowest possible risk for the salesperson, with a cap on long-term earnings. Commissions and bonuses tend to be modest, and the level of security, at least if we think in terms of a monthly paycheck, is relatively high.

I know there are many variations and compromise positions between these extremes. Remember, I am talking about basic principles here. Remember that neither package is "right" or "wrong" in and of itself. Your job as a manager is to align one of these two approaches to a specific salesperson, based on his or her experience.

The low-risk, low long-term income potential package probably will be the best for those people who are just beginning in a given field or just starting their career in sales. Take this approach with people who are not yet ready for huge fluctuations in income, and who have the potential to grow within the position. (Remember the "corporate career turning point"—frequently, salespeople will bail out of a sales position because they conclude that the perceived risk of the monthly income picture is too high. We could fix that problem by starting a brand-new salesperson with a lower-risk package.)

The other payment package—the one that has high risk and higher reward, which may entail dramatic income shifts from month to month and quarter to quarter—is best for someone with a good deal of experience. Offer this package to someone who may view the absence of long-term income-earning potential as a personal or career disadvantage. (Some people might even consider it an insult.) If one of your salespeople falls into the "experienced and proven" category and is offered a compensation package that minimizes risk and maximizes month-to-month stability, she may feel constricted and may start looking elsewhere for opportunities. By the same token, if someone is just getting started in a given field and is eager to maintain a certain level of income stability—and perhaps, to impress parents and relatives and associates with his ability to make it on his own—the high-risk, high-income package is not likely to be very attractive. If you insist on sticking with the wrong compensation package for someone, don't be surprised when that person moves to another team, perhaps even to a competitor!

Training and Retention

Once you have identified the people on your staff you would most like to retain, your job is to develop training and retention programs that will encourage those people, your top performers, to stay with the team.

You'll recall that training constitutes a major portion of the eight-week coaching plan discussed elsewhere in this book. I've encouraged you to use the Fifteen Coaching Points checklist to develop training events; you may want to build training programs around the personal and professional development goals you identify in your top people.

What will your top-tier people in this group buy into? What's the best format for giving them the kind of training and coaching they're looking for? How can you keep them engaged? What's the best way to get them to conclude that you know they are making a valuable contribution to the organization? How can you get these people visibility (if that's what motivates them)? Public and private recognition plays a huge role in retention of key salespeople, as do the right professional challenges.

Whatever training program you choose, *spend some time developing it and reinforcing it after it is executed to ensure that the key points stay with your people.* The vast majority of salespeople receive little formal training over the course of a year, and reinforcement of the training they do receive is virtually nonexistent. All too often, managers get distracted with emergencies and overlook the benefits of a training program—namely, retaining key people and hiring better sales members for the team as a whole.

Not long ago, one of the trainers at my company was asked by the senior vice president of sales, "What happens if the top people on our staff implement your ideas, prove their skills, and then decide to move to another company?"

Our trainer looked at him for a moment and then said, "Let me answer that question by posing another one. What happens if you *don't* train your people and your *least* effective people *don't* change what they are doing and they decide to *stay*?"

You can learn more about the training and retention options my company can offer for your team by going to page 257, or visiting our Web site at *www.dei-sales.com.*

When Should You Fire Someone?

One thing I've learned over the years is that when sales managers ask about one thing, they may not realize that they are actually asking about something else.

For example, when a sales manager asks me to help his team to improve closing skills, I have learned, from long experience, that what is actually happening is that his team needs help with the information-gathering portion of the sale. If we help with that portion, we will automatically improve the team's closing ratios. But I don't have a magic wand or special formula to give salespeople for the end of the sales cycle, even though sales managers sometimes like to think such things exist. They may *diagnose* the problem as a closing skills problem, and from a certain point of view they may be correct, but helping the team focus on improvements to closing techniques is a little like trying to teach a fast-food attendant working the window at the local Burger King how to make better career choices. You have to start earlier in the process. Similarly, when sales managers ask me about when to fire salespeople, the issue at hand is not really about firing or turnover. All too often, the question is not one of when to let a salesperson go, but how to prevent people with habitual performance problems from becoming permanent employees. That needs to happen, in my experience, within three weeks of a hiring decision. You read that right. *Three weeks.* That's when you should recognize that there's a problem and let the person go. Not six months later or a year later. For the record, I want to share here, in a nutshell, my philosophy on firing salespeople. It is this: *Do it very early, or do it as an absolute last resort.*

I am challenging you to identify the people who are *unlikely* to make a meaningful contribution to your organization. I am challenging you to identify them very early in the employee cycle. I am challenging you to get rid of them then.

After that point, your goal should be to do everything to *keep* your salespeople on the team. Once somebody makes it past that initial window, *do everything you possibly can to hold on* to that person. You have trained this employee, offered emotional support to this employee, and exposed your prospect base to this employee. It should be a last resort kind of decision to let that person go, even if there is a temporary performance problem.

Of course, if the performance problem shows signs of being more than temporary, or if there are major problems like serious insubordination or drug abuse, you have little choice: You must begin working with the Human Resource people to lay the groundwork for letting this person go. But let's face it: Most of the time, that's not what we're looking at.

That's why I want to draw your attention, not to the end of the process, but to the beginning of the hiring cycle, in the hope that you can minimize later problems and reduce overall turnover by taking more effective action in the front end of the cycle. In our organization, we let people go if they do not produce within three weeks.

That's all the time they have to show me they're on the right track. Three weeks.

When I share this fact with sales managers, they sometimes stare at me in disbelief. There is an important footnote to add, however. When I say, "produce" within three weeks, I am not necessarily talking about closing a sale. What I am talking about is setting a sufficient number of *first appointments* to eventually deliver a sale.

To repeat: They don't have to *close* a sale within three weeks. They have to *set appointments* during the first three weeks. Or I fire them.

Why wouldn't I? What would be different, if I decided to stick with the person after three weeks of not setting appointments? What could I expect to change in this person's approach to the job? *Setting appointments is what I'm hiring them to do.*

Take a close look at what I am saying. Listen to what I tell salespeople upfront when they decide to sign on with my organization. I tell them: "Look, I have certain expectations from you. This early ramp-up period is very important to me, and I hope it is important to you. I want to be very specific about my expectations. My expectations are that you are going to hit the phones hard, right away, and that you will set up initial meetings with at least fifteen people over the next two weeks, and with at least five new people each week after that. Now, I'm going to be very honest with you and tell you that if you do not hit these targets, your job is going to be in jeopardy. If you *do* hit the targets, and I know you can, I will work with you to make sure that they move forward in a way that will get you the income you are looking for."

That's the contract.

Think about the effect that having a conversation like that would have on your overall turnover rates. Somebody who decided to stay with your company after that kind of talk would almost certainly be highly motivated to develop the first appointments you want. On the other hand, somebody who could not make that commitment to you, or made the commitment and then didn't take action on it, would probably be the kind of person you would end up firing anyway. So, doesn't it make more sense to get that second group of people out of the way early, rather than investing months and months of training time with them?

I have mentioned certain specific activity targets—fifteen meetings after two weeks, five meetings in the following week—that correspond to my industry and my sales cycle. You will have to establish your own benchmarks for *your* industry and *your* sales cycle. What I want to leave you with now is the notion that *shooting straight with your recent hires will increase the likelihood of their sticking around over the long term and will dramatically reduce the chance of your having to fire anybody later on.*

The challenge is to be direct enough in your communications early in the process to insure that you get productive results later in the process.

What about the problem performer who nosedives after putting months or years in with your company?

My advice here is to do everything you possibly can to retain this performer. Sometimes that will not be possible. But if there is even a glimmer of a chance that a series of intensive one-on-one coaching meetings will help turn him or her around . . . if there is even a glimmer of hope that a few weeks off might help give him or her a new lease on life . . . then I urge you to do that rather than let the person go. There will certainly be some situations where these options are not realistic, but my philosophy is and always has been to try to work with salespeople through challenges and crises to improve their long-term prospects within the organization. Short-term connections with salespeople are nice, but they do not deliver the long-term results, both financial and strategic, that having seasoned professionals on your team will deliver. If you can, find a way to hold on to the person.

Improving Time Management Skills

Here is the single best way to turn someone around who you might otherwise have to fire.

Improve the Team Member's time management skills.

Everyone goes through phases in his or her career, and salespeople are no exception. My experience is that senior salespeople sometimes fail to do what they used to do intuitively—namely, manage their own time effectively. If you can work with the person to help her improve daily time management skills, you may stand a better chance of holding on to a contributor you've spent months or years developing.

Exceptionally poor time management is a sign of a career crisis. The failure to track one's time closely and carefully *as it is actually spent* is a major obstacle to identifying specific performance problems. In my coaching sessions, I recommend that salespeople evaluate their working day extremely closely and then make a radical and conscious series of changes in the very next day's schedule. I recommend this step because I believe that obsession without evaluation of habits results in chaos. (That is another way of saying obsession without discipline results in chaos.)

To me, discipline is the act of evaluating your own habits and changing them if they are not working. Chaos produces a very negative stressful, outcome and is likely to lead to burnout among your team members. Helping the person make incremental improvements in time management skills, on the other hand, helps prevent burnout.

Proven Time Management Principles for Salespeople

Build these principles into your coaching sessions:

Get the person to start each day early. Some salespeople claim that they are not "morning people." If you want to buy into this, you can, but the fact is that the business world really does operate from about 8:00 A.M. to about 6:00 P.M. in our culture. If your staff member is consistently giving away half of that day because he or she shows up late and does not really start getting into action until 11:00 or so, you have to find a way to change that habit.

Get the person to set a goal and evaluate the day against it. Have your salesperson identify a particular sales-related goal that is important to him and that he is working hard to obtain. For instance, the salesperson might choose the goal of closing six new sales this month so that he can take his wife on a vacation to the tropics. Now have the person take a brand-new notebook and keep track, for one full day, of *everything*—and I do mean *everything*—he does on the job. Make sure he writes it all down. Use fifteen-minute increments and make the person list the most important things he did during every fifteen-minute period. At the end of the day, have your salesperson look at the time log—or better yet, sit down and go over the time log together. Put a plus sign by activities that end up moving the sales-person closer to the goal he has identified. Put a circle by activities that had no effect whatsoever on whether he moved closer to the goal. Put a minus sign by activities that actually ended up moving the person away from his goal. Now ask the salesperson these questions:

- How many different things did you do during the day?
- When did you do them?
- Is that when you planned to do them?
- How does what you accomplished compare with what you wanted to accomplish?
- How much time did you allocate to each task?

- Were there ever times when you were "busying yourself" with activities that had no effect whatsoever on whether you moved forward to your goal?

- How else could you handle these activities? Could they be delegated or eliminated from your day?

- Were there ever times when you spent time on activities that actually moved you away from your stated goals? What were you doing during these times? Are you going to do the same thing tomorrow? If so, why?

- What conclusions can you draw about what you did today? What should you be focusing more of your time and energy on?

- How does what you learned about your day affect your priorities for tomorrow?

You want the salesperson to understand, at a gut level, the difference between being *busy* and being *productive*. Many mediocre salespeople are extremely busy. But high achievers are extremely productive.

Sometimes salespeople press you on the difference between "busy" and "productive." For my staff, I know and can define that difference. You should know the same for your staff. Set specific criteria.

Here are the only four scenarios that qualify as a productive day at my company, D.E.I. Management Group:

1. I scheduled a first appointment with somebody.

2. I moved an existing prospect forward as evidenced by that prospect's willingness to sign a contract or set aside a specific date and time to talk to me within the next two weeks.

3. I "touched" a current or former client (by making a phone call, sending out a mailing, sending a personalized e-mail, etc.).

4. I did any combination of 1, 2, or 3.

Anything else is not a productive day by D.E.I. Management Group standards; instead, it is a busy day!

Send the message: "Keep track of how you use your time." *Help* your salespeople keep track of how they are using their time. With somebody you are considering getting rid of but want to retain, I would suggest performing this exercise at least once a week and asking the earlier questions in a collegial, nonthreatening manner.

Other principles you may want to keep in mind for effective time management coaching include:

Encourage the salesperson to cluster similar activities together. Yes, your salesperson will be interrupted during the day. That does not mean his or her priorities should change in a heartbeat. Encourage the person to try to gather similar activities into the same chunk of the day.

Help the salesperson plan two weeks in advance. Your salesperson should know, today, what his or her major priorities are going to be for each of the next ten business days.

Send the message: If you manage your own time effectively, you can (and should) be your own boss. Your salesperson really should set his or her daily priorities to reach the sales goal you've both worked together to identify. Your salesperson should know his or her own weaknesses and take responsibility for improving them. Your salesperson should set intermediate goals and know what rewards will inspire action. Ultimately, this stuff should be less your job, and more of the salesperson's job!

Forty Habits That Waste Your Organization's Time

Here's a checklist featuring forty common time-wasting habits, based on our studies of over 750,000 business professionals all over the world in virtually all industries. Review the list and see how many bad habits show up in your office. Which of these habits is keeping you and your people from being as efficient as possible?

Planning

____ **1.** Consistent lack of objectives/priorities/written daily plan.

____ **2.** Perpetual crisis management/perpetually shifting priorities.

____ **3.** Attempting too much at once/unrealistic time estimates.

____ **4.** "Waiting" (for planes/appointments, etc.) without filling the time with productive activity.

____ **5.** Impatient/inability to stick to a given plan.

Organizing

____ **6.** Personal disorganization/cluttered desk.

____ **7.** Confused responsibility/no chain of command or authority.

____ **8.** Duplication of effort.

____ **9.** Multiple supervisors on projects where there should only be one.

____ **10.** Paperwork/red tape.

____ **11.** Poor filing system.

____ **12.** Inadequate equipment/facilities.

Staffing

____ **13.** Untrained/inadequate staff.

____ **14.** Understaffed.

____ **15.** Overstaffed.

____ **16.** Absenteeism/tardiness/turnover problems.

____ **17.** Poor attitude among personnel/personal problems distracting from work.

____ **18.** Staff overly dependent on supervisor/inability to make decisions or coordinate effectively or act independently.

Directing

____ **19.** Ineffective delegation/over-involvement in routine details.

____ **20.** Lack of motivation/indifference.

____ **21.** Coordination/teamwork.

Controlling

____ **22.** Constant interruption from telephone/letting ringing phone run your day.

____ **23.** Constant interruptions from drop-in visitors.

____ **24.** Inability to say no.

____ **25.** Incomplete/delayed information.

____ **26.** Lack of self-discipline.

____ **27.** Habit of leaving tasks unfinished.

____ **28.** Lack of standards/controls/progress reports.

_____ **29.** Excessive visual distractions.

_____ **30.** Excessive aural distractions (noise).

_____ **31.** Not enough information about current projects.

_____ **32.** Key people consistently unavailable for discussions.

Communicating

_____ **33.** Meetings go on too long.

_____ **34.** Unclear communication/instructions/lack of instructions.

_____ **35.** Excessive socializing/idle conversation.

_____ **36.** Talking too much.

_____ **37.** Failure to listen effectively.

Decision-Making

_____ **38.** Procrastination/indecision.

_____ **39.** Demanding *all* the facts—as opposed to all the *necessary* facts—before making decisions.

_____ **40.** Making decisions with little or no information.

What Has to Happen Before You Fire a Salesperson *after* the Initial Probationary Period?

"Yeah, but when do I actually fire somebody who's been on staff for a while?"

Ten sales problems have to show up in the salesperson's daily routine before I will fire that person.

Remember, we are not talking about a new hire, but about people who have passed that three-week probationary period. Here are my ten warning signs, from years of experience, indicating that a salesperson needs to be let go. Again, all ten need to be in place for me to terminate the person.

1. Failure to make prospecting calls on a daily basis, not for just one day, not for just one week, but for a period longer than that, and despite ongoing coaching in this area.

2. Failure to track personal ratios, not just occasionally but for a protracted period and after having been coached in this area.

3. Inventing excuses to do something other than sell. Again, not just occasionally but as a daily coping skill. (*Note:* Not long ago, I spoke to a sales manager whose salespeople were supposedly selling advertising via radio slots. She told me that three of the people on her staff had, for the past month, refused to make any prospecting calls, because they were too busy developing copy for the advertisements that would run for their current customers. Instead of trying to negotiate your way out of a situation like this, change the structure. Hire somebody whose job it is to write the copy, make the photocopies, deliver the mail, make the

coffee, whatever—and insist that your salespeople focus on what you hire them to do, namely, selling.)

4. Failure to master or understand the company's success stories. This is inexcusable. If a seasoned salesperson is unfamiliar with the company's recent successes and is unwilling to learn or discuss those successes, there is a serious problem.

5. Lack of confidence, not just in one area but in lots of things. Salespeople who fall into this category appear to have lost, not just their confidence, but also their identity. They're looking around for who they really are. They are afraid, for whatever reason, of being turned down.

6. Failure to ask directly for the Next Step while they are in a meeting. This dangerous habit is easier for a veteran to fall into than you might imagine. Despite how good the relationship with the prospect is, your salespeople need to get their prospects, whether they are long-term contacts or people they just met this morning, to open up the appointment book and schedule a date or time for some future interaction.

7. Being too passive or too aggressive. Sometimes, you get the sense that a person is simply walking through the day, waiting for someone else to point him in another direction. If you see that the person who reports to you is finished selling, but simply has not admitted it to himself or herself, that is a serious problem. The flipside of this, of course, is aggression and/or insubordination on the job. Either insolence or extreme passivity is a serious warning sign.

8. Failure to hit quota, not just in one performance period but over a protracted period. One bad quarter is not a good reason to fire someone.

9. Failure to communicate with you, the manager, about what's happening in the territory—not just once, but over a protracted period.

10. Failure to plan the day intelligently, not just once in a while, but as a regular workplace reality. If the salesperson does not even try to put together a to-do list, and always deals with issues as they come up without ever setting priorities for the day, that is a serious problem.

Take a close look at that familiar final warning sign: time management. My experience is that if you can actually make measurable progress in the area of time management, you will find that many, or most, of the other nine warning signs will begin to improve "on their own." (I put that phrase in quotes because time management is a key to just about everything else on the list—confidence, income performance, ratio management, and so on.)

When I encounter someone who displays all ten of these troubling warning signs, I do not waste time. I sit the person down, look him or her in the eye, and say, "We've got to talk." I then close the door, ensuring that we have privacy, and I lay the bad news on the line.

"This is not working out. It's time for both of us to move on."

I keep the meeting short and try to avoid emotional exchanges. The message is painful, so there is no need to add excess emotion to the discussion. Explain what has happened, listen, but do not change your decision. Set the timetable for the person's departure, and move on.

Special Notes for Managing Telesales Teams

Most of the coaching principles in this book are very easily adapted to the world of the telesales professional, but there are a couple of additional points that deserve to be mentioned because they are unique to this work environment.

First, if you are a telesales manager, you do not need me to tell you that certain types of work that fall into this category can be extremely stressful. This is not true of every telesales work environment, but it is true of those teams who reach out to cold contacts and turn them into customers. (The exception, in my experience, is the professional whose job it is to maintain relationships and occasionally "upsell" to someone with whom he or she already has an established series of business connections. For this group, selling over the phone is less a matter of short-term persuasion, and more along the lines of long-term alliance building and occasional updates.)

When I am working with telesales teams that must interact many times a day with people they have not met, I make a point of emphasizing that I know what they are doing is one of the very hardest types of selling. This is so because:

- They cannot see the people to whom they're selling.

- They have to be better prepared, in many cases, than the field salesperson does.

- They hear more and harsher "no" answers than just about anybody else.

- They are more closely observed by management.

■ They have long-term compensation challenges that may or may not be directly addressed by their managers. (I know this may be a sensitive topic, but my instinct has always been to address it directly, rather than to pretend that it does not exist.)

If you address these issues openly with your salespeople, explain that you really do understand why what they do can be a challenge, and ask for their input on the best ways you can both work together to handle the challenges they face, you will be setting yourself ahead of the vast majority of managers of telesales teams. If you go even further, and institute a regular coaching program along the lines described in this book, you will almost certainly be in the top 1 percent of telesales managers in your industry.

Instituting regular coaching meetings is only part of the picture, however. The question of encouraging salespeople to monitor their own numbers is a good deal more complex in the telesales field, because there are more variables to measure. Here is a sample Numbers Overview that we use when training telesales people to begin monitoring their own daily numbers: Perhaps you can use a model along the same lines to help your people track their activity.

⇩

Outbound sales process starts here   Inbound sales process starts here

# of call attempts	# of discussions	# of interviews	# of proposals / presentations	# of sales offerings	# of "by the way" upsell attempts	# of upsells
	100	81	74	40	11	1

It may also be interesting to ask your team to give you a brief summary, in writing, of the last three sales each person closed and the number of discussions it took to close the sale. (Obviously, you will want to exclude brand-new hires from this exercise.)

By evaluating the results, you should be able to get fairly close to a figure that will identify your average selling cycle—not necessarily in terms of calendar days, but in terms of the number of meaningful discussions your people have before closing the deal. I want to share here one of the more important success stories we have ever had at my company, which was related to this exercise. We asked one of our clients to conduct this poll with their telesales team and found that the vast majority of deals were being closed by the third call.

The problem was that most discussions with prospects continued into the fifth or sixth call. That is to say, the majority of the telesales team members were violating the principle of not investing time and effort past the average duration of the sales cycle, unless extraordinary circumstances suggested they should do so. Armed with the information that the typical sale closed in three calls and that the typical telesales' team member was placing five and six calls to the same person without generating a sale even though those calls did ultimately generate a sale, we made a blindingly obvious suggestion: Stop calling the fourth time.

By insisting that the telesales team *move on to someone new* after the third attempt to discuss their sales offer, we were able to post a double-digit increase in their total revenue in a very short period. My sense is that this principle could benefit many telesales organizations around the world, not just the ones we have trained.

Try it!

Challenges for Telesales Professionals

There are many different kinds of telesales professionals, but most of them have one thing in common, at least in the United States: They are going through a difficult passage. They face increasing regulation and even public hostility toward their profession. Major news stories and political campaigns these days are built around fomenting hatred of telesales professionals!

Telesales is an honorable way to make a living, and people who choose this line of work deserve to be treated with dignity and respect. I also believe that they deserve advice on how to succeed over the long term in their chosen line of work. Here are some strategies designed exclusively for these team members; please consider sharing them with your people.

Accept that telesales is a fundamentally different way of making a living than other kinds of selling, and acknowledge that the "rules of the road" as they apply to telemarketing professionals are going to be a little different. *How you think about yourself and your job are vitally important.* If you follow the simple steps you're about to read, you will be in a much better position to pace yourself, make the most of your phone interactions, and match what you offer to what is really happening in the lives of your prospective customers. And you'll be happier and less stressed-out on the job.

Schedule the telesales day differently. The question of how to approach the day for telesales professionals is particularly important.

Field salespeople can break up their day or week with off-site visits to prospect offices and trips to tour their facilities. Most telesales professionals can't, and that can be a significant problem. Because they operate in this different environment, telesales professionals have to keep some specific points in mind as they schedule their day. Here are some points to consider.

Do not try to run a marathon. In other words, you should certainly block out portions of your day, and fill them with bursts of calling activity. But you should also break the day up with periods of less intense, less emotionally challenging work. You might, for instance, choose to spend half an hour making a certain type of call and clustering together all the outbound calls that you can. You might then schedule half an hour to review e-mails, update your contact base, and so on, before returning to calling activity. Warning: If you are tempted to try to multitask, don't—it never works! Do not try to make calls at the same time that you manage your paperwork or do other tasks. When you are doing outbound calls, focus on the calls alone. Because the potential for stress and burnout is so very high, you should either be "on" or "off"—at least when it comes to making outbound calls. You should not attempt to be "kind of on" all the time.

Do not call for too long. Try to make your calls between forty-five and fifty minutes each hour; then take a break and do some other activities during the other period.

Keep calling right after you have had a bad call. This may seem counterintuitive, but by postponing the next call after somebody beats you up, you increase the likelihood that you will postpone placing the next call, or dread it when you do place it. You are a professional. Like a doctor or a lawyer or a professional football player, you sometimes face situations that are challenging and/or disorienting. But that doesn't mean that you withdraw into a little cocoon while you are still in your on-the-job "prime-time" mode!

Personalize your telesales interactions. Try to "humanize" the call. By this, I mean to find a way to draw parallels between what is going on in your world and what is going on in the prospect's world, even if doing so, is not entirely sales-specific. So, for instance, if you are selling magazine subscriptions, at some point during the call, you may want to mention the fact that your own children enjoy reading a magazine you represent that is designed for young people. This kind of person-to-person approach can go a long way toward reducing the incidence of burnout-inducing stress you experience during the course of the average day.

Schedule a daily workout. Of course, this is a good idea for everybody, but it is a particularly relevant and important step for telesales professionals. Telesales can become a very sedentary job if you let it, and the "fight or flight" syndrome can be particularly dangerous to your outlook if your job description requires you to sit in one spot for a great deal of time and talk to people who may be hostile. Break the pattern. Get outside for a walk or a jog during lunchtime or some other period.

Oil the equipment. Your voice is everything! Keep a glass of water nearby to keep your composure and keep your throat and mouth moist.

Always ask the other person what's changed in his or her world. This is particularly important on incoming calls. If someone contacts you to place an advertisement designed to sell a motorcycle, you should ask the person what made him or her decide to call you in the first place. After all, the person didn't call because there was nothing better to do. Did the person recently decide to move to another city? If so, are there other items he or she is interested in selling? By asking about the motivation for the call, or about what took place recently in the other person's world, you will gain meaningful information. By citing parallels between the other person's recent experiences and your own, you can also do a better job of "humanizing" the call.

Invest in personal and professional development. Get in touch with my organization, D.E.I. *(www.dei-sales.com),* and arrange for a free subscription to our newsletter, the "Executive Sales Briefing." This quarterly newsletter features many articles of interest to telemarketers.

One final note to managers of telesales teams: The Prospect Management System I have outlined in this book has a column for First Appointments, which is located to the left of the 25 percent column. Many telesales managers have asked me how they can use the system when their people do not schedule fact-to-face meetings. The answer is actually quite simple, and remarkably consistent across virtually all telesales selling environments: Instead of measuring First Appointments, measure what I call Initial Contacts, or ICs, in the same column. What is an Initial Contact? It is the second "good conversation" that your salesperson has with a contact. This column, Initial Contacts, will drive the entire sales triangle in the same way that First Appointments drive the Prospect Management System for field sales representatives.

What We Figured Out in This Section

- Once you identify the most common factors for sales success on your team, and paint a portrait of what your ideal performer looks like, you will have a much better idea of what qualities you should be looking for in your next hire.

- Compensation plans fall into two broad categories: *all upside, high risk* or *no risk, low income, low long-term income potential*. The first usually works better for experienced performers, while the second usually works better with newer salespeople.

- You need to establish *within three weeks* of hiring whether a salesperson can do the job. Regarding firing salespeople, the best philosophy is this: *Do it very early, or do it as an absolute last resort.*

- The single best way to turn someone around whom you might otherwise have to fire is to improve his or her time management skills.

- Telesales is fundamentally different from other kinds of selling, with a different set of challenges and a different type of stress that you will need to take into account and learn how to manage.

APPENDIX

Resources for Sales Managers

In this part of the book, you will find a variety of articles and resources, many of which you can share with the team in order to enhance specific skill areas. Use them!

Fifteen Critical Selling Principles

by Stephan Schiffman

1. Always respond to customers and prospects within forty-eight hours. Why on earth wouldn't you?

2. Schedule sales appointments for early (8 A.M.) or late (4 P.M.). This is the single best time management strategy for salespeople.

3. Follow through immediately on thank-you letters, letters of agreement, and internal paperwork. What message do you send to customers, prospects, and superiors if you are habitually late in these areas?

4. Set two new appointments every day. If you do, you will not lack for prospects. Guaranteed.

5. Strategize with your sales manager on a regular basis. Ask for help—and be ready to use your boss as an advocate within the target organization.

6. Don't kid yourself. You can't be a superior salesperson and make a habit of self-deception about prospects and customers.

7. Create a sense of urgency in all your communications. This is your job, and no one else's.

8. Be honest. People won't give you repeat business if they don't trust you.

9. Know ten client success stories. Be ready to share them at the drop of a hat.

10. Decide on your opening question for the meeting. Don't walk into the meeting without a plan!

11. Decide on the Next Step you want and ask for it directly. This, too, is your job, and no one else's.

12. Always get the prospect to do something. Another meeting. A visit to a facility. A conference call. Something has to land on the other person's calendar, preferably for a slot within the next ten business days.

13. Don't obsess on a single account.

14. Don't call the same person to try to set a face-to-face meeting more than once a week.

15. Don't invest a lot of time and energy in a relationship where the other person has invested little or nothing. This is particularly important. I worked with one woman who boasted that she had visited a single account thirty-three times before closing. That may sound impressive. But what if the time she spent on that call could have been devoted to prospecting efforts? Those prospecting calls would probably have led to two sales—or perhaps considerably more.

The Nine Principles of Cold Calling

Here are the nine proven principles that will support a successful cold calling campaign in virtually any industry. Follow them!

1. **Rather than set a daily "number-of-dials" goal, set the goal for the number of first appointments you want to maintain** at all times. As you learn more and more about your conversion ratios (see principle 3), make the adjustments that make sense for you to achieve your activity and income goals.

2. **Make cold calls daily with the objective of setting at least one new appointment every day.** This does not include networking meetings. Block the time out and call for an uninterrupted period. Don't send e-mail or receive incoming calls during that block. Approach this activity with discipline and a sense of urgency.

3. **Begin tracking your dials, completed calls, and appointments set on a daily basis right now.** Compile your results daily; benchmark your activity to assess your success and help determine your true ratios.

4. **Do not stop dialing if you are not meeting with success.** Stand up, take a break, practice, reread this article—do whatever you have to do, but don't stop. If you are calling within a particular industry and are finding appointment making tough, diversify your leads.

5. **Always be prepared to cold call. Have an identified lead list ready with you always, and use it when you have unexpected time available.** Don't let organizational issues get in your way. Do not research or prioritize your calls between calls—your calling time is your peak sales time! Do that work "off-peak."

6. **Learn the appropriate third-party references.** Briefly reference your company's past and current success stories—but don't let a lack of complete knowledge keep you from making calls. Don't promise you can do the same thing for this prospect as you did for the ABC Company. Instead, ask for a meeting so you can learn more about the person's unique situation and share what you did with ABC Company.

7. **Practice each aspect of the calling process until you are comfortable and confident with your approach.** Prepare for the specific objections you will hear, and be more ready to turn them around than the other person is to brush you off. When in doubt, say, "You know, a lot of people told us that before they saw how we could. . . ."

8. **Ask directly for the appointment.** If you haven't asked for one meeting at one specific date and time during the course of the call, you aren't doing it right.

9. **Don't kid yourself.** Sales come from prospects and prospects come from appointments.

The Next Step:
An Overview

by Stephan Schiffman

In selling, a Next Step is tangible evidence that someone is working with you—playing ball with you. It's not a gut feeling that the person is interested in playing ball with you, but proof of that interest.

At D.E.I., where I work, we believe that interest is demonstrated by action. That action takes the form of an agreement to meet with you, speak to you, or do something for you typically within the next two weeks. This is the Next Step.

Six Reasons to Fight for a Next Step

Reason 1: It Shortens Your Selling Cycle

At the end of a sales meeting, most salespeople say "I'll call you in a week or two." They end up wasting all kinds of time playing phone tag. Why not set the Next Step while you're still face-to-face? You can save one to three weeks between each meeting—and perhaps as much as a month off your overall sales cycle. (And you can save time every day by avoiding phone tag, too.)

Reason 2: Territory Management

Once you know you are meeting again with this client, you can set another appointment in the area. You can work *in advance* to set up other meetings. This contact may be more likely to meet with you at hard-to-fill time slots (8:00 A.M., 4:00 P.M.) than someone you have no rapport or history with.

Reason 3: Time Management

Fact of sales life: The proposal that's due "sometime next week" will probably slip to the bottom of your priority list. The proposal that's due because of a meeting you've scheduled for next Tuesday at 2:00 will be less likely to slip. Find out exactly when it's *due* so you know when to *do* it. Why? Because there are three priorities you should always make a conscious effort to schedule: meetings with prospects, work you have to do *before* a meeting with a prospect, and prospecting time.

Reason 4: You'll Know Who to Follow Up With

Let's say it's a busy month. Maybe you have twenty first appointments in a busy month. Say that seven of them don't go anywhere—you get a clear *no* or the person is obviously unqualified. If you don't ask for a Next Step at the end of the first meeting, that means thirteen people are in "call-me-next-week-sometime" mode. What if you also have thirteen people like that from *last* month . . . and thirteen from the month before that? But suppose you only have time for five quality proposals this month. Whom do you focus on? Well, if you regularly ask for a Next Step, you know *exactly* who to write a proposal for: the people who agree to a Next Step! Remember: Interest is demonstrated by *action*. You are prioritizing people who agree to Next Steps because at least they agreed to see you again. The others, when asked, *didn't* agree to see you. So here's the question: If they didn't agree to *see* you, what makes you think they'll *buy* from you?

Reason 5: You'll Send the Right Message

Translation: Your time is valuable, too. Consider this: We teach people how to buy from us. So we don't want to say, "When are you free?" but rather: "I've got a slot at eleven on Tuesday, does that work?" Sending the "When are you free?" message is professional suicide. Why would you want to send someone the message, "I'll travel two hours out of my way to spend two minutes with you"?

Reason 6. You Worked Too Damn Hard to Set Up the Appointment in the First Place

You've made a sizable time investment to set this up, drive out, and meet with the prospect. Why walk away from that without a commitment?

Sixteen Ways to Ask for a Next Step

---

1. **When You Want to Get Corrected** (This is probably the simplest and most effective Next Step strategy.)

   "I think this meeting went well."

   "Here's why I think it went well. I think I see a possible match between what you're trying to accomplish and what we do."

   "So, let me tell you what I think we should do."

   "I want to come back here on Tuesday at two and show you an outline of how we might be able to work together, based on what we've talked about today. Does that make sense?"

2. **When You've Hit a Technical Obstacle**

   "Let me come back here on Tuesday at two and introduce your tech people to my tech person."

3. **When You Want to Escalate the Sale**

   "I get the feeling I should meet your boss. Why don't you and I meet with him on Tuesday at two?"

4. **When You Want to Escalate the Sale (Variation)**

   "I really get the feeling your boss ought to meet my boss. Let's set up a meeting. How's Tuesday at two?"

5. **When You Want to Gain or Regain Access to Key People**

   "Let's meet with your team for an hour—so we can all work together to build the proposal for you. How's Tuesday at two?"

6. **When You Want to Reassure the Prospect**

   "Let's have a meeting with Happy Customer. You really ought to talk to him. How's Tuesday at two?"

7. **When You Want to Position Yourself as a "Virtual Employee"**

   "I've got an idea. Why don't I talk to your team about what they're doing, and do a little free consulting for you? I'll give you my analysis. We should really set up a date for me to report to you. How's Tuesday at two?"

8. **When the Prospect Is Having Trouble Visualizing the Benefit of What You Sell**

   "I've got an idea. Why don't you come by and sit in on one of our programs/training sessions/other customer event. How's Tuesday morning at eight?"

9. **When You Want to Improve Your Relationship by Spending Time at a Neutral Site**

   "I've got an idea. We have tickets for a special industry event/trade show, and I'd love you to be there and see it. How's Tuesday night at eight?"

10. **When You Want to Exchange Access to Their People for Access to Your Product**

    "I've got an idea. Why don't I set up a demonstration for you and your boss so you can see how this product works? How's Tuesday at two?"

11. **When You Want to Help Them Visualize How You Can Benefit Them**

    "I've got an idea. Why don't you come by and visit our facilities so you can see how we work and meet our key people. How's Tuesday at two?"

12. **When You Want to Reassure Them That You Understand Why They're Different**

    "I've got an idea. Why don't I take a tour of your plant and see it firsthand. How's Tuesday at two?"

13. **When You Want to Rescue a "Fallback"—a Dormant Lead**

   "I've been thinking about the plan we put together for you, and I'm not happy with it. I have a new plan I want to show you. May I come by Tuesday at two?"

14. **When You Want to Rescue a "Fallback"—a Dormant Lead (Variation)**

   "I was just thinking of you. We really ought to get together again. May I come by Tuesday at two?"

15. **When You Want to Rescue a "Fallback"—a Dormant Lead (Variation)**

   "I'm going to be in the area, I'm meeting with XYZ Company. We ought to get together again so I can see what you're doing. May I come by Tuesday at two?"

16. **When You Want to Rescue a "Fallback"—a Dormant Lead (Variation)**

   "I have an idea I want to discuss with you. May I come by Tuesday at two?"

   Finally, remember this . . .

   Whatever the situation, the Next Steps you suggest must be:

   - Clear

   - Perceived as helpful

   - Easy to agree to

   If you don't get a Next Step when you ask for one, it may be because you're suggesting something that is hard to understand, is not perceived as helpful, or is difficult to agree to.

The Elephant and the Salesperson: Five Questions You Can Use on Your Next Sales Call

So, this salesperson walks into a prospect's office and notices that there's a large elephant standing there in the middle of the room. He stares at the elephant, looks at his prospect, then takes a seat, pulls out his brochure, and pretends there's no elephant.

It sounds like a joke. But it's deadly serious. In fact, it's the most common obstacle to effective selling today.

While there are many questions that salespeople have been taught to ask, few relate to the elephant. Most salespeople never ask a question about the elephant. In fact, it's even worse: Most people *train themselves* to ignore the elephant.

How can this be? Well, the typical salesperson has a short set of prepared questions to begin the selling session. That salesperson is convinced that those five or six memorized questions are the best questions to ask at every meeting, whether they are open-ended or closed-ended questions. But a quick look at the average results of asking those questions suggests that a different approach to interviewing might be more effective.

What is the one thing that a salesperson knows when he or she walks in the door to see someone for the first time? The person's name? Maybe. The person's title? Maybe. The company's product or service? Maybe.

But there's something else.

The one thing that we salespeople can count on—the one critical fact we know for sure—is that this customer is not ours. That's the only meaningful thing we know. That's the elephant. So why don't we *ask* about that at the beginning of the meeting?

The number-one competitor, for the majority of salespeople, is the status quo. In other words, the real competition is what the prospect is doing now by force of habit. That's what matters. They do not "need" us, no matter how many need-based questions we may choose to ask. Frankly, if we went out of business tonight, few people would care.

So. If we know that the true competitor, the status quo, is standing there like an elephant in the middle of the room, why don't we ask *that* question?

Here are five questions that will help you to uncover your real competition, the status quo:

1. I checked my records, and I noticed that you are not working with us. I'm just curious, whom you are using now?

2. Is there a reason that you've chosen to use (Company X)?

3. Can you tell me how you use the product/service? How does the end-user work with the product/service?

4. When was the last time you reviewed the product/service? (This question assumes that you don't know of any immediate problem with the product/service. If you do know of a problem, ask about that.)

5. I think that we're better than (Company X), but I can't prove it if I don't know how you made the decision to go with them. Why did you decide to work with that company?

Instead of questions that ignore the elephant, try these simple questions on your next sales call . . . and see if you don't get better results.

Three Principles
for Effective Time
Management

Effective time management skills make all the difference in sales. If you develop them, you can keep your life in balance. If you don't, you will constantly feel stressed, behind schedule, and (probably) sleep-deprived. That last problem is particularly serious, since no salesperson who is a victim of constant insomnia is likely to perform well at work.

My experience is that the failure to track your time closely and carefully as it is actually spent is a major obstacle to diagnosing specific time management problems. One of the steps I recommend to any salesperson who is feeling cynical about his or her profession, or about sales work in general, is to evaluate a working day very closely and then make a radical, and conscious, series of changes in the next daily schedule. I recommend this step because of my belief in a principle that I consider a golden rule: "Obsession without evaluation of habits results in chaos."

When we feel that we have no sense of control over our day—when we have no clear indication of cause and effect, of how one thing we do positively affects an outcome in another area—then we are the victims of chaos. When we seem to be driven by circumstances rather than driving them, we are the victims of chaos. When our daily schedule never allows us any time to evaluate exactly what the daily activities actually led to, then we are the victims of chaos.

So, what do you do to avoid chaos? Evaluate your habits. Find out what outcomes those habits are actually delivering for you. Are they taking you closer to your goal, or moving you farther away from it?

Step One: Know Your Outcome

To start with, identify a particular sales-related goal, one that's important to you and that you're willing to work hard to attain. (For instance, you might choose the goal of closing six new sales this month so that you can take your spouse on a vacation to the tropics.)

Step Two: Track Your Time

Now take a brand-new notebook and keep track, for one full day, of everything you do on the job. Write it all down. Use fifteen-minute increments and list the most important thing you did during each period.

Step Three: Analyze

At the end of the day, look at your time log. Put a plus sign next to any activities that ended up moving you closer to your goal. Put a circle next to activities that had no effect on whether you moved closer to your goal. Put a minus sign next to activities that actually ended up moving you away from your goal.

- How does what you learn about your day—about what's working and what's not—affect your priorities for tomorrow?
- How many different things did you do during the day?
- When did you do them?
- How much time did you allocate to each task?
- Were there ever times when you were busying yourself with activities that had no effect whatsoever on whether you moved toward your goal? How else could you handle these activities? Could they be delegated? Could they be eliminated entirely from your day?
- Were there ever times when you spent time on activities that actually moved you away from your stated goal? What were you doing during those times?

There is, we must always remember, a big difference between being very busy and being very productive. Many mediocre salespeople are extremely busy.

High achievers are extremely productive. Use this simple exercise for a full day at least once every month to help you set priorities and build schedules that put you in the "productive" category!

Words to Live By

Here are some thoughts to help you and your team respond resourcefully to challenges that may come up. Consider posting these, one at a time, on a company bulletin board on a rotating basis.

"Always know in your heart that you are far bigger than anything that can happen to you."—Dan Zadra

"All great ideas are dangerous."—Oscar Wilde

"Knute Rockne liked 'bad losers.' He said 'good losers' lose too often." —George Allen

"Everything's in the mind. That's where it all starts. Knowing what you want is the first step toward getting it."—Mae West

"The ultimate measure of a man is not where he stands in moments of comfort and convenience, but where he stands at times of challenge and controversy."—Martin Luther King Jr.

"I like thinking of possibilities. At any time, an entirely new possibility is liable to come along and spin you off in an entirely new direction. The trick, I've learned, is to be awake to the moment."—Doug Hall

"If one advances confidently in the direction of his dreams, and endeavors to live the life which he has imagined, he will meet with a success unexpected in common hours."—Henry David Thoreau

"I long to accomplish a great and noble task, but it is my chief duty to accomplish small tasks, as if they were great and noble."—Helen Keller

"Trouble is only opportunity in work clothes."—Henry J. Kaiser

"Keep true, never be ashamed of doing right. Decide on what you think is right, and stick to it."—George Eliot

"You miss 100 percent of the shots you don't take."—Wayne Gretzky

"Never underestimate the power of passion."—Eve Sawyer

"Nothing happens unless first a dream."—Carl Sandburg

"When written in Chinese, the word *crisis* is composed of two characters. One represents danger and the other represents opportunity."—John F. Kennedy

"Intelligence without ambition is a bird without wings."—C. Archie Danielson

"I've learned that when someone is looking sad, or says something bad happened, never say, 'What's the matter?' or 'What's wrong?' Always say, 'Do you want to talk about it? I'm here for you.'"—H. Jackson Brown Jr.

"Never give up on what you really want to do. The person with big dreams is more powerful than the one with all the facts."—H. Jackson Brown Jr.

"Reach high, for stars lie hidden in your soul. Dream deep, for every dream precedes the goal."—Pamela Vaull Starr

"Surmounting difficulty is the crucible that forms character."—Anthony Robbins

"Throw your heart over the fence and the rest will follow!"—Norman Vincent Peale

"To conquer fear is the beginning of wisdom."—Bertrand Russell

"A well-spent day brings happy sleep."—Leonardo da Vinci

"Always do right. This will gratify some and astonish the rest."—Mark Twain

"Happiness is the sense that one matters."—Sarah Trimmer

"In the long run, people only hit what they aim at."—Henry David Thoreau

"Try not to become a man of success but rather try to become a man of value."—Albert Einstein

"We are what we imagine. Our very existence consists in our imagination of ourselves. The greatest tragedy that can befall us is to go unimagined." —N. Scott Momaday

"Work and play are the same. When you're following your energy and doing what you want all the time, the distinction between work and play dissolves."—Shakti Gawain

"You can gain strength, courage, and confidence by every experience in which you really stop to look fear in the face. You must do the thing which you think you cannot do."—Eleanor Roosevelt

"You don't get to choose how you're going to die, or when. You can only decide how you're going to live. Now."—Joan Baez

"Experience is not what happens to a man. It is what a man does with what happens to him."—Aldous Huxley

"You may have a fresh start any moment you choose, for this thing we call failure is not the falling down, but the staying down."—Mary Pickford

"Nothing great was ever achieved without enthusiasm."—Ralph Waldo Emerson

"Remember your dreams."—Maryanne Radmacher-Hershey

"Whatever is worth doing at all is worth doing well."—Lord Chesterfield

"When you follow your bliss . . . doors will open where you would not have thought there would be doors; and where there wouldn't be a door for any-one else."—Joseph Campbell

"You can if you think you can."—George Reeves

"Experience teaches only the teachable."—Aldous Huxley

"Yes, risk taking is inherently failure-prone. Otherwise, it would be called sure-thing-taking."—Tim McMahon

"One can never consent to creep when one feels the impulse to soar." —Helen Keller

Resources for Handling Stress

Sometimes, borderline performers just need a little help in mastering the art of distancing themselves from things that seem larger than they actually are. Getting some perspective on what really matters is the first step in transforming unproductive, internalized stress into productive, action-inspiring stress. In addition to pointing team members toward my book *Beat Sales Burnout: Maximize Sales, Minimize Stress* (Adams Media), you may also want to suggest that they visit one or more of the following sites:

About.com—Stress
http://stress.about.com
Stress, stress-induced conditions, and managing stress, including research on medical conditions related to stress and tips for its control and management. Also self-assessment tools, articles, links to hundreds of choice sites.

Alternative Stress and Relaxation Solutions
http://stress-management.net
Stress, relaxation, and stress-relief solutions and information including personal counseling and corporate programs. Links to other stress-relief therapies, products, and programs.

The American Institute of Stress

www.stress.org

Details ways to identify and manage stress effectively.

Preventing and Curing Employee Burnout

www.employer-employee.com/Burnout.html

Tips and strategies for preventing burnout for managers and employees.

Fifteen Coaching Points Checklist

Use the worksheet that follows to analyze and rank every member of your team.

I strongly recommend that you do this at least once every quarter, and that you build your personnel evaluations around progress in the fifteen performance areas identified in this form.

Fifteen Coaching Points

Team member name _____ Date _____

> **Zero to five total check marks: Level Three Performer (assume 25% of total value of "live" prospects will turn into revenue)**
>
> **Six to ten total check marks: Level Two Performer (assume 33% of total value of "live" prospects will turn into revenue)**
>
> **Eleven to fifteen total check marks: Level One Performer (assume 50% of total value of "live" prospects will turn into revenue)**

Energy: Setting First Appointments

____ 1. **Understands own ratios.** Is the salesperson monitoring activity ratios on a daily basis? What do the ratios look like? What specific ratio improvement would you like to see?

_____ 2. **Has time to complete call targets.** Is prospecting a top priority on the average selling day? Does the salesperson make time to complete prospecting activities on a daily basis?

_____ 3. **Number of calls/day steady.** Is the salesperson consistent, or are there (for instance) zero prospecting calls for five straight days, followed by thirty or forty calls the next selling day?

_____ 4. **Adequate appointments each week.** Is the number of _new_ meetings consistent from week to week? Is it the right number, given this person's ratios?

_____ 5. **Each first appointment (FA) takes no longer than thirty minutes to set.** How long does it typically take this salesperson to set a first appointment?

Sales Efficiency: The Sales Process

_____ 6. **Understands closing ratio.** How many meetings or discussions does it take this person to produce a single sale? Is that the right ratio? Can the salesperson discuss this ratio intelligently with you?

_____ 7. **Timeline and sales cycle understood.** What is the average selling cycle on this salesperson's most profitable product/service? Is the salesperson capable of identifying this number without getting distracted by "exceptions" that turned into sales? Does the salesperson understand that what _usually_ happens determines his or her selling cycle?

_____ 8. **Process-oriented (doesn't waste time with dead leads).** Does this salesperson know when to move on?

_____ 9. **Masters product knowledge/ product malleability.** Can this salesperson make the product or service fit in a number of different situations or environments? Has this salesperson ever targeted an entirely new category of prospects?

_____ 10. **Takes between sixty and ninety minutes to set and prepare for each follow-up appointment.** Does this salesperson get parallel commitments and input from the prospect _before_ committing large amounts of time and energy to proposal development?

Value Efficiency: Price Proposition

____ 11. **Understands pricing structure and margins.** Can the salesperson explain to you the company's margin on what he or she sells? Does the salesperson understand why the different products and services cost what they do?

____ 12. Able to **propose a price that is close to the contract price.** How close is the pricing in the first draft of the proposal to the final pricing?

____ 13. **Takes long-term view of account.** Does this salesperson know when and how to use strategic pricing and bundling skills to close an initial pilot deal with an important prospect—and still make money for the company?

____ 14. **Negotiates from strength, not weakness.** Does the salesperson avoid the trap of discounting without getting something in return? Does the salesperson live by the rule that you should never, ever offer a discount before a customer asks for one?

____ 15. **Handles price issues honestly and forthrightly.** Does the salesperson stand behind his or her company's pricing, and answer questions directly and with integrity?

About the Author

Stephan Schiffman is a certified management consultant and the founder of D.E.I. Management Group, a global sales training company. Mr. Schiffman has helped more than 500,000 professionals become more successful through a variety of selling and coaching programs. He is the country's pre-eminent expert on sales prospecting, and the author of many popular business titles, including *Cold Calling Techniques (That Really Work!)*. To learn more about Stephan Schiffman or D.E.I. Management Group, call 1-800-224-2140 or visit *www.dei-sales.com*.

Training Programs Available from D.E.I.

The following sales training programs are available from Stephan Schiffman's company, D.E.I. Management Group. For information on these programs, call 1-800-224-2140, or visit *www.dei-sales.com*.

Appointment Making

This full-day program prepares salespeople to increase appointments with decision-makers. Participants learn and practice all of the skills associated with appointment making:

- Using ratios/metrics as a diagnostic tool and as a foundation for action planning.

- Understanding the real role of prospecting as a component of sales success.

- Creating the right calling approach for each lead source.

- Anticipating and handling objections.

- Creating turnarounds that effectively overcome all objections and questions and lead to appointments.

- Practicing the skills that build confidence.

- Learning all the proven strategies that enable salespeople to get through to the decision-maker.

- Learning the improvement tips that lead to ongoing improvement and success.

Prospect Management

This full-day program teaches salespeople a systematic method for evaluating, categorizing, prioritizing, and strategizing all of their opportunities, appointments, and prospects using a proven visual-tracking system. Participants leave the class with a real-time view of their inventory of prospects (as opposed to suspects) and can strategize more effectively.

Participants learn:

- The difference between a prospect and a suspect.

- How steps and time of sale accurately predict sales success.

- How to differentiate between opportunities and true prospects.

- Strategies to consistently practice effective time and territory management as well as efficient selling techniques.

- How to organize their opportunities into a simplified visual-tracking system.

- How to coach themselves.

High-Efficiency Selling Skills

This one- or two-day program teaches salespeople the skills associated with selling efficiently. Participants learn:

- How to articulate value statements and product/company differences.

- How to conduct first meetings that lead to Next Steps.

- Improved interviewing and presenting skills.

- Next Step strategies that enable participants to maintain momentum, shorten sales cycles.

- How to role-play in order to rehearse important upcoming meetings.

Telesales

This one- or two-day program teaches salespeople who sell over the phone to use proven techniques to open discussions and close sales more effectively. This program is adjusted for inbound, outbound, and hybrid phone/field salespeople. Participants learn:

- A calling model to ensure success and increase confidence.

- The importance of ratios in order to hit ever-increasing goals.

- The Two Critical Points—enabling callers to get past initial objections as well as secure Next Steps.

- How to articulate value and differentiation statements.

- How to conduct phone interviews that sound like conversations.

- How to role-play in order to rehearse important upcoming calls.

Coaching to Build Sales Momentum

This one- or two-day class teaches managers of sales teams how to coach effectively in order to change sales and work habits and help the team meet or exceed ever-increasing sales goals. Participants learn:

- The many factors that block salespeople from being successful.

- How to implement a proven coaching model.

- How to deal with common "problem" personalities.

- How to role-play to rehearse actual upcoming coaching sessions and increase manager confidence.

- How to more effectively conduct one-on-one and team sales meetings.

- How to approach long-term goals through a series of eight-week action plans.

Advanced Interviewing

In this one-day program, participants learn how to use body language, "right" question framing techniques, improved listening skills, and Next Step/relationship building strategies to improve their overall communication skills *and* the quality of their information to the customer. Participants:

- Are challenged to reveal what they know (and don't know) about their key accounts.

- Learn an interview model approach enabling them to engage the customer more consistently in conversation.

- Learn a new, higher standard of information necessary to advance sales and maximize account value.

- Learn how to "gauge" and "engage" the customer.

- Practice advanced interviewing techniques and increase confidence in new skills.

Presenting/Public Speaking

In this one-day program, participants find out about the art of presenting to groups. Participants learn:

- A checklist for Pre-presenting, and Post Presenting in order to ensure consistency of success.

- Several effective presentation opening techniques.

- Strategies for effectively dealing with committees.

- A simple model for effectively structuring all speeches.

- How to engage an audience.

- How to deal with difficult audience members.

- How to role-play to rehearse actual upcoming presentations and increase confidence.

Sales Negotiating

In this one-day program, participants learn how to negotiate more effectively in order to close profitable sales while improving and expanding relationships. Participants learn:

- How to use a proven sales negotiation model to ensure consistency of success.

- How to verify information initially collected in order to present "right" (winning) proposal.

- Proven successful negotiating strategies.

- How to avoid common negotiation mistakes.

- How to bundle/articulate offers in a variety of creative ways that increases the perceived value of the offering.

- How to understand customer's mindset before and during negotiation process.

- How to role-play to rehearse actual upcoming negotiations and increase confidence.

Major Account Selling

In this one-day program, participants find out how to map key accounts in order to develop action plans around prioritized opportunities. Participants learn:

- How to use a simple, visual mapping tool to fully exploit opportunities within key accounts.

- What they know (and don't know) about the opportunities and decision-makers within their accounts.

- How to gather the information, prioritize opportunities, track progress, and achieve account growth.

- How to proceed with actionable strategies within each account they are attempting to grow.

Persuasive Business Writing

In this one-day program, salespeople and others in the organization overcome the most common business grammar and style problems, and learn to make all their written communications. Participants learn:

- How to improve e-mail messages.

- How to develop a powerful written proposal.

- How to build a powerful visual presentation with PowerPoint.

- How to use the written word to win interest and commitment.

Index

A
Appointments, 103–5, 125–26, 139

B
Behaviors, 40, 71–73, 147–60
Burnout, 31–32

C
Career stages, 41–43
Change, 38–43
Closing deals, 10, 61–64, 80–84, 87, 98–105, 140–41
Coaches, 33–37
Coaching concerns, 134–38
Coaching model, 28–29
Coaching plan, 184–90
Coaching points, 125–31, 253–55
Coaching sessions, 145–46, 161–71, 175–83
Coaching strategies, 143–46
Cold-calling principles, 235–36, 243–44
Communication principles, 59, 89–90, 144–45
Compensation plans, 207–8
Competitor, 75, 244

D
Discipline, 19–20
Discrepancies, 47–54

Dollar line, 1, 11–12

E
Efficiency, 34–35
Energy, 9–10, 34–35, 123–26
Expectations, 11–14, 25–29

F
Family issues, 16–17, 71–73
Firing salespeople, 211–13, 221–23
"First Appointment," 103–5, 125–26, 139
Forecasting, 55–56, 128–30
Forms, 171, 179–83

G
Goals, 25, 31–32

H
"High-stress" selling, 91–92
Hiring salespeople, 26–27, 195–97

I
Income, 1, 11, 207–8
Information-gathering, 82–84, 87
Interviews, 5–8, 201–6

L
Lead generation, 53